Zanzibar Style
recipes

Published in 2003 by
Gallery Publications
P.O. Box 3181, Zanzibar
email: gallery@swahilicoast.com

London office:
32 Deanscroft Avenue
London NW9 8EN
email: zjafferji@aol.com

© 2003 Gallery Publications
Photographs © Javed Jafferji
Text © Gemma Pitcher
Illustrations © Pascal Bogaert
Graphic Designer: Antony Chunguli
Designed by Zanzibar Gallery Publishers

ISBN 9987 667 22 8

Dedicated to my aunts Kulsum and Batul Jafferji, who
always make good food.

Other books in this series:
Zanzibar Style:
Voted one of the 'Top 20 travel books for Christmas
2001' by the UK's Times newspaper.
Safari Living:
Showcases Tanzania's top safari lodges and camps.
Safari Living Recipes:
Recipes from the cream of Tanzania's bush chefs.

Cover picture: Mnemba Island, Zanzibar.

Zanzibar Style
recipes

Photographs by Javed Jafferji
Edited by Gemma Pitcher
Styling by Kulsum Jafferji

Gallery Publications

Contents

The East

The North

Islands

Pemba

Introduction

How would you like your meal, sir? Reclining on a cushion and gazing over the rooftops of the ancient Stone Town? Bobbing gently on the deck of an ocean-going dhow as the sun sets behind the sultan's palace? Or perhaps stretched out in the shade of a palm tree, watching the fishermen dragging their catch up the beach?

From scraps of cassava roasted over charcoal to cauldrons full of aromatic pilau rice served up at lavish weddings, food is consumed with gusto everywhere in Zanzibar and her sister island, Pemba. The islands' famous spices combine with hundreds of fruit varieties and a wealth of fish and seafood to create a uniquely delicious and distinctive cuisine little known in the rest of the world.

Zanzibar's position on the edge of the Indian Ocean has brought visitors from other lands since time immemorial - Persians, Chinese, Arabs, Indians and many more have all sailed their vessels into Zanzibar's harbour over the centuries, bent on trade and sometimes plunder. And with these strange visitors came new ways of eating - heaps of glass noodles from China, sweetmeats from Arabia, spices from India. Zanzibar's cuisine, like its language, is a mix of ingredients from all over the world.

These days the visitors that arrive in Zanzibar are bent not on trade or piracy, but on relaxation, indulgence and a revival of the spirit. International travellers have become connoisseurs, able to circumnavigate the globe with ease in search of the finest, most decadent experiences the world has to offer. Zanzibar is now firmly established as one of the world's most exotic destinations, and the visitors that arrive here have high expectations to be fulfilled. They are not disappointed. Zanzibar's hotels and restaurants combine Eastern hospitality with Western flair, providing standards of design and cuisine the equal of any of the world's better-known playgrounds.

This collection of recipes is intended as a testament to Zanzibar's culinary abilities. The hotels and restaurants who allowed us to share their secrets are among the best in the world, and their chefs are artists in their own right. We hope you enjoy following in their footsteps.

Stone Town

No culinary attraction in Zanzibar can beat an afternoon spent strolling around the streets of the island's capital, Stone Town. There's something of interest round every corner – a a lunch café in a tiny, paved garden, serving simple rice and meat among the old neem trees, accompanied by the sound of prayer from a nearby mosque. Or perhaps one can catch a glimpse of an old man in a flowing white kanzu strolling along with a brass coffee pot yoked over his shoulders, counterbalanced by a tray of little china cups. At Darajani market, a riot of colour, noise and smell, symmetrical piles of oranges, peppers or spices lie tantalisingly alongside chunks of fish, all arranged under palm-thatch shelters. Here ragged men wheel bicycles groaning under the weight of banana-leaf baskets, honking an old-fashioned car horn endlessly to advertise their wares of young green coconuts, newly-caught octopus or live, clucking chickens.

Cassava, Zanzibar's staple food, is roasted on open barbeques and sold with a twist of *pili-pili* - chilli salt - in an old piece of newspaper. Sugar cane juice sellers energetically work the handles of old-fashioned mangles, pulping the long fibrous stalks over and over into a bucket of ice among a cloud of wasps. At dusk, another old man quietly takes his place on a street corner, the scent of new-baked bread wafting from under the lid of his basket, and like ghosts, the dignified figures of veiled ladies emerge from their doorways and flit across to buy his wares.

Blues Restaurant

One of Zanzibar Town's most prominent features since it was built on a jetty jutting out into the harbour, Blues is one of Zanzibar's most popular eating and drinking spots. No matter how hot and humid the narrow stone streets of the old town become, Blues can always be relied on to provide a haven of tranquillity, cool shade and excellent cooking. The bright green waters of the Indian Ocean twinkle through the slats in the floorboards, tiny fish, attracted to the glowing lanterns, congregate at night around the legs of the jetty, and the smells and sounds of the nearby food market filter gently in on the sea breeze. The interior design of Blues goes for a carefree, nautical feel, with bright blue canvas or comfortable wicker chairs and polished wooden tables.

Lunchtimes at Blues are always busy, with a wide variety of excellent snacks, salads and pasta dishes on offer. Succulent fish and seafood, cooked to local as well as international methods and imaginatively presented, is on offer for dinner. Later in the evening the bar often hosts lively parties for Zanzibar's community of expatriates, with lethal cocktails being mixed by the friendly staff.

Zanzibari prawns and calamari with a spinach and coconut sauce

Serves 1

Spinach and coconut sauce

100g shallots

2 tbs curry powder

1 tsp turmeric

1 tsp ginger fresh

1 tsp garlic

100ml fish stock

150ml coconut milk

salt and pepper

200g spinach, blanched and chopped

Heat oil in the pan, add shallots and fry without colouring. Add all spices, ginger and garlic. Stir well then pour over fish stock and reduce by 1/4. Then add coconut milk and spinach.

Deshell the prawns and cut the calamari into rings. Pan fry prawns and calamari until half cooked, then pour the sauce over the top and season. Cook until creamy and thick, season and serve with pilau rice.

Changu (Dorado) fish stuffed with fish mousse

Serves 1

1 raw whole Dorado fish, gutted

For the fish mousse:

300g of white fish - Dorado or any firm fleshed white fish

2tbs crème fraiche

1tbs of chopped parsley

1 egg

Fresh coriander

2 tsp curry powder

Blend all the ingredients together until mousse is firm in texture.

Run a knife down the spine of the whole fish, taking care not to damage the skin. Carefully roll the flesh back from the bones, making sure no bones are left inside. Using scissors, cut the spine behind the head and once again in front of the tail and ease the spine and ribs out. Alternatively, ask the fishmonger to do this for you. Then fill the fish with mousse using a soup spoon.

Put the fish on a baking tray and arranged halved tomatoes around it together with some fish stock and sliced onions. Cook in the oven at 150° for 2 hours, making sure the fish does not dry out. Remove and serve with pilau rice.

Swahili seafood curry

Serves 4

Vegetable Curry:

4 green peppers

2 carrots

2 onions

2 courgettes

500ml coconut milk

2 cloves

2 cardamom

1 stick cinnamon

1tsp cumin

2 tbs curry powder

2 tsp turmeric

4 tsp garlic crushed

4 tsp ginger crushed

1 small bunch fresh coriander, chopped

Seafood mix:

600g calamari

800g boneless kingfish fillet

400g fresh tuna

16 king prawns, headed and deveined

200g octopus

1dl fish stock

Cut fish and vegetables into small cubes. Roast and blend cloves, cardamom, cinnamon and cumin.

Put all seafood except calamari in a pan. Add the fish stock, cook for a few minutes, then add calamari, simmer for 2 minutes, then strain the stock and keep the seafood aside.

Heat oil in a frying pan, add first carrots and onions, cook for 2-3 minutes then add green pepper and courgettes, fry softly. Add garlic, ginger, curry powder, turmeric and all spices, mix well. Add seafood stock, bring to the boil then add coconut milk, simmer until cooked to your liking and thick enough. Season, mix in seafood.

Serve sprinkled with coriander in a coconut husk.

Forodhani Gardens

No visitor to Zanzibar can avoid eventually wandering into the hustle and bustle of Forodhani, an enormous seafood market on the harbourfront. Here the smoky glow of petrol lamps and charcoal braziers illuminates neat piles of squid, marlin, octopus, lobster and tuna for the benefit of a parade of wide-eyed tourists, sassy beach boys and coy, kohl-eyed adolescent girls.

In addition to the heaped mounds of seafood, samosas, crusty naan breads and delicious sweetmeats, the major culinary delight of Forodhani is known as Zanzibar pizza. Zanzibar pizza is actually more of a combination of omelette and pancake, with the pizza chef flipping their neat blobs of dough onto the hot skillet with a showmanlike flourish that would do justice to a European pastry chef serving up *crêpes suzette*.

The chefs are flamboyant characters, showmen through and through, who whirl their circles of pizza dough above their heads while shouting out banter to the gaggles of women, platform shoes peeking incongruously from their black, all-enveloping veils, who pause by each stall and eat the deliciously crunchy, buttery squares of dough with delicate relish.

onion, coriander and chopped green chillies to the prepared meat. Keep aside. Stretch the dough balls into a very thin circle on a chopping board or metal surface. Make sure the edges are thinner than the centre. Put 2 tablespoons of the prepared meat mixture in the centre of the circle. Break eggs on top of the meat and close the circle by bringing 2 sides up over the other two sides, folding into a square. Put one teaspoon of oil on a medium hot griddle and bake this envelope over a low heat on both sides until the egg is cooked. Repeat this process with the remaining dough. Cut into four squares and serve with salad and tomato chutney.

Zanzibar pizza

Serves 6

100g plain flour

Pinch salt

120ml water

240ml oil

450g finely minced meat

1 tsp garlic paste

3-4 fresh chillies, diced

1 onion, finely chopped

2 stalks fresh coriander, chopped

6 eggs

Salt and pepper to taste

Sieve the flour into a bowl, add salt and enough water to make a smooth dough, and knead for 2-3 minutes. Divide the dough into 6 equal balls and put in a shallow dish. Pour the oil over them, making sure they are well coated. Then cover and put on one side for 2 hours.

Mix the minced meat with the salt, pepper, garlic and ginger paste and fry, stirring continuously until the meat is cooked. Allow to cool and then add the finely chopped

Sesame bread

Serves 6 to 8

900g plain flour

1 sachet yeast

480ml coconut milk

2 eggs

2 tbs sesame seeds

salt

Sieve the flour into a bowl and add all the ingredients except the sesame seeds. Mix and knead to make a smooth dough. Cover and leave in a warm place to rise for half an hour. Divide the dough into small balls. Pat each ball into a round shape between the palms of your hand and then pull one side to make a teardrop shape. Sprinkle with sesame seeds and cook lightly on both sided under a grill or on a griddle.

Mishkaki

Serves 6

1350g diced beef, chicken (or goat!)

1 tbs red chilli powder

1 tbs ginger paste

1 tbs garlic paste

1 tbs tomato paste

2 tbs cooking oil

Salt and pepper

Mix all ingredients in a large bowl and marinade the meat overnight, or for at least four hours, in the fridge. Prepare your charcoal fire, place the meat on the skewers and grill. Baste occasionally with oil and brush with chilli sauce. Serve immediately on paper plates, accompanied by chips, chapattis or sesame bread.

Vegetable sambusa (samosas)

225g plain flour

1/2 tsp salt

1 cup water

1 cup oil

175g potatoes, boiled and cut into very small cubes

175g vegetables (carrots, peas, spinach), chopped

1/2 tsp garlic

1 tbs oil

1 onion, finely chopped

1tsp garam masala

2-3 green chillies, chopped

4 stalks coriander, chopped

salt and pepper

Sieve the flour into a bowl, add salt and enough water to make soft dough and kead for 2-3 minutes. Divide the dough into four equal balls. Using a chopping board or a flat surface, roll each ball evenly into a circle of about four inches in diameter. Spread each circle evenly with oil then sprinkle flour over the top of the oil. Place each circle on top of the other and repeat. Gently roll out the layered circles into a large circle of about 8-9 inches in diameter. Using an iron griddle or frying pan, very lightly fry each circle on both sides without using any oil. Leave to cool. Cut the layers into 3 strips and peel off the pieces to make 12 sambusa. Keep the strips under a damp tea towel.

Mix the vegetables with the salt, pepper and garlic and cook on a medium heat with 1 tbs oil for 5 minutes until the vegetables are soft. Allow to cool, then add all the remaining ingredients and keep aside to fill the sambusa pastry. Take one strip of pastry, fold it together to form a cone and stuff with a teaspoon of prepared filling. Fold the pastry over and around the filling to form a triangle, and deep fry until golden.

Kidude

Born Fatuma Binti Baraka in the early years of the 20th century, Bi Kidude's musical career started in the 1920s, when she walked from place to place across the length and breadth of what is now Tanzania, performing at traditional Taarab concerts. Taarab is the ubiquitous music of the Swahili Coast which combines the violins, ouds and ganoons of the Arabic tradition with the drums and flutes of Africa. These days, Bi Kidude is the undisputed queen of Taarab in East Africa, an international superstar whose presence at a wedding or state occasion commands attention and respect.

As befits a Zanzibar institution, Bi Kidude now even has a restaurant named after her. The deliciously air-conditioned Kidude café, next door to Emerson and Green Hotel, offers a welcome reprieve from Zanzibar's heat and humidity. The full bar is cleverly set amongst beautiful art, handicrafts and Zanzibar antiques, with vibrantly patterned batik cushions line the traditional stone baraza benches around the walls. Modern artistic and photographic portraits of Bi Kidude's proud, impassioned face complete the decor.

The eclectic lunch and dinner menu at Kidude is inspired by the old slave trade countries of the Indian Ocean: Arabia, Africa, the Caribbean and even the Cajun cuisine of the Americas.

Pumpkin coconut soup

Serves 4

1 tbs butter

50g onion, finely chopped

200g cooked pumpkin

652ml chicken stock or water

375ml milk

1/8 teaspoon ground cloves

1 tsp fresh grated ginger

1 tsp lemon juice

1/2 tsp cinnamon

A dash of Tabasco

1/2 tsp salt

250ml coconut milk

125ml cream

Heat the butter over moderate heat, and cook the onion for about 5 minutes until soft but not brown. Add the cooked pumpkin, stock, milk, spices, lemon juice, Tabasco, and salt and simmer for 15 minutes. Add the coconut milk and cook for one minute longer. Puree the soup in a blender, and then stir in the cream. Be careful when blending hot liquids, fill only 1/4 to 1/2 full at time. Blend in batches if necessary.

Prawn creole

Serves 6 to 8

6 tbs unsalted butter

1 large onion, halved and finely sliced

1 large sweet green pepper, halved, seeded, and thinly sliced

2 celery stalks thinly sliced

2 cloves garlic thinly sliced

1 bay leaf

2 tsp paprika

200g tomatoes, peeled, seeded, and diced

250ml tomato juice

4 tsp Worcester sauce

4 dashes Tabasco sauce

salt

1 1/2 tsp corn starch

800g shrimp, shelled and deveined

Steamed rice to serve

Melt 2 tablespoons butter in a frying pan and fry the onion, green pepper, celery and garlic for 1 or 2 minutes. Add the bay leaf, paprika, tomatoes, tomato juice, Worcester and Tabasco sauces. Bring to the boil and reduce heat. Simmer and reduce liquid by a quarter until vegetables are soft. Mix corn starch and a little warm water to form a paste, and stir into the sauce. Stir sauce for 2 more minutes and remove from heat.

In another frying pan, sauté the shrimp in remaining butter for 2 to 4 minutes depending on the size. Reheat the sauce and add the prawns and cook for one more minute to heat the prawns through. Serve with rice and garnish with fresh herbs and lemon.

Pineapple upside-down cake

Serves 8

185g all-purpose flour

170g sugar

2 tsp baking powder

1/2 tsp salt

60ml vegetable oil

180ml cup milk

1 tsp vanilla

1 egg

1 lime, grated rind

1 tbs fresh lime juice

55g butter

85g dark brown sugar

1 fresh, ripe pineapple

Preheat the oven to 175°C. In a mixing bowl, sift the flour, sugar, baking powder and salt. Add the oil and milk to the bowl and beat for one minute. Add the vanilla, egg, lime rind, and lime juice, blending just until well combined. In a cast iron skillet, or large frying pan, over medium heat, melt the butter. Remove from the heat and sprinkle the brown sugar around the skillet. Arrange the pineapple slices around the base of the pan. Pour the batter evenly over the top of the pineapple, and bake for 45 minutes. Remove from the oven and cool the cake in the pan for 5 minutes. Turn the cake out onto a circular   platter.

Baked fish in parchment with crab sauce

Serves 4

Four fillets of kingfish, or any tender white fish, 200g each

5 scallions or 1 bunch of chives

1 clove of garlic, minced

2 tbs butter

2 tbs flour

225g crab meat

60ml white wine

250ml milk

Heat the butter over low heat and sauté the garlic and green onion gently until soft, be careful not to brown them. Add the flour and cook stirring for about two minutes. Add the milk and cook until the sauce thickens. Add the wine and the crabmeat and heat thoroughly. Place each fillet on a sheet of baker's parchment paper, and top with the crab sauce. Fold into a package, and bake at 200°C, for about 7 to 10 minutes.

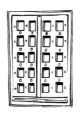

Mercury's

Freddy Mercury, Zanzibar's most famous citizen, was born Farouk Bulsara on the 5th September 1946, to parents Bomi and Jer Bulsara. Both Freddy's parents were of Indian and Persian descent, members of the ancient Zoroastrian religion. His father, Bomi, was a civil servant, working as a High Court cashier for the British Government.

In 1954, at the age of eight, Farouk was shipped to India to attend boarding school. The newly named teenage 'Freddy' arrived back in Zanzibar in 1962 and completed his last two years of education at St Joseph's convent school. He spent his free time swimming on Zanzibar's beaches or cycling around the island with his friends. In 1964 the Bulsaras, along with many other Zanzibaris of Indian descent, left the island in the wake of the revolution, never to return.

Mercury's restaurant, on a tiny corner of beach close to Stone Town's commercial port, is a tribute to the rock singer's colourful life and his hard-living style. The extensive bar is open all day, serving a variety of lurid and lethal cocktails along with generous portions of seafood, hearty soups and satisfying pizzas. The décor features various portraits of the great man himself as well as a large almond tree growing through the roof!

Dafu (young coconut)

Konyagi 60ct (can substitute any fierce local gin!)
200ml young coconut juice (find a small boy to climb your coconut tree for you!)

Take Konyagi, ice cubes and coconut juice put them all together in the coconut shell.
The beauty of simple things...

Prawn masala

Serves 8
1/4 kg butter
2kg jumbo prawns
1/2kg chopped onion
1/2kg tomato
1/2kg tomato puree
Masala powder
200ml yoghurt
Small bunch coriander
100g garlic
1/2 litre vegetable stock

Boil peeled prawns until half cooked. Toss onion and garlic until brown and add fresh tomato and tomato puree, after 2 minutes add yoghurt and Zanzibar masala powder, add prawns and stock and allow to boil for 10 minutes. Put the prawn masala in the bowl and garnish with coriander.

Served with steamed basmati rice and fresh market vegetables.

Zanzibarian mix

Serves 1
2 fresh bananas
30cl Bacardi
60cl Malibu

Put all ingredients in the blender together with ice cubes and blend for 1 minute.
Serve in a highball glass.

Freddie Mercury deep blue

Serves 1
60cl Blue Curacao
20cl Bacardi
30cl Malibu
100ml pineapple juice

Take all ingredients in the shaker together with ice cubes. Shake it until very cold, pour into a straight beer glass.

Wacha kujiregeza

Serves 1
30cl Tia Maria
30cl Ballantines
30cl Amarula cream liqueur

Put all ingredients in a tulip glass with crushed ice.

Bull's eye pizza

Serves 8

1600g spicy pizza dough

1l fresh tomato sauce

250g grated mozzarella cheese

350g slices peeled potato

100g slice onion

100g green pepper

100g sliced tomato

8 whole eggs

Form the dough into round shapes (8pcs) put fresh spicy tomato sauce on top, arrange potato slices, onion, sliced green pepper and sliced tomato. Cover with grated mozzarella cheese and top whole egg at the center of the pizza. Put it in the oven for 8 minutes. Take it out, brush with butter, cut into 6 slices.

Tembo House Hotel

A prominent feature of the Stone Town waterfront, the Tembo was once the headquarters of a wealthy Zoroastrian merchant. Today the magnificent white buildings, renamed the Tembo House Hotel, hold one of Zanzibar Town's best loved and most characterful hotels.

The Tembo's interior design is rich in history and distinctly Indian in style, with Isamaili red and green stained glass windows and exquisitely carved darkwood furniture. The black and white marble floors follow a trend set long ago by followers of the Omani sultans. The Tembo's pleasant, shady dining room is also known as the Bahari restaurant, open to the sea on one side, and furnished with local antiques. Sunsets are magnificent when viewed from here, and the menu features local cuisine, prepared to traditional Swahili methods, alongside more international fare.

All the bedrooms at the Tembo are spacious, and beautifully decorated with oriental and traditional Zanzibari ornaments, antiques and furniture. The hotel's swimming pool, surrounded by coconut palms, is a welcome place to cool off during the heat of the day while watching dhows sail past on their way into the harbour.

minutes and then cover with aluminum foil and leave with cook in the over at moderate heat (230 - 250F)

Sweet banana

Serves 1

4 small sweet bananas
1l coconut gravy
6 cardamom seeds
1/2 tbs sugar

Grate the coconut flesh and pour over 1 cup of water, then squeeze it through a piece of muslin, to get a thick liquid. Mix this with the pieces of sweet bananas and add the rest of the ingredients, then let it cook for 15 minutes.

Plain pilau

Serves 4

1kg basmati rice
2 onions sliced
2 garlic cloves
2 ginger cloves
Few cinnamon sticks
10 cardamon pods
1 bunch dill
1/2 l cooking oil
1l beef stock
1/2 tsp table salt

Clean the basmati rice, put oil in a pot and heat, then fry the onion slices till brownish. After that add the beef stock and the remaining ingredients with salt and let it simmer for 10 minutes. After this add the rice, cook for 20

Chuku chuku curry

Serves 6

6 slices of kingfish
2 potatoes
2 tomatoes
2 onions
2 lemons
1/2 tsp table salt
1/2 tsp turmeric

Cut the kingfish into 6 slices then put in a saucepan, add chopped potatoes, tomatoes and onions. Add the turmeric then boil for 5 minutes. Add salt and lemon to taste. Remove from heat and serve.

Green banana in coconut sauce

Serves 4

1 bunch green bananas

1l coconut gravy

1 onion

2 tomatoes

1/2 tsp turmeric

1/2 tsp table salt

2 lemons

Grate the coconut flesh and pour water over it, squeeze it through a piece of muslin. Mix the thick liquid with pieces of green banana and add chopped tomatoes and onions.

Add turmeric, salt to taste and lemon to make seasoning. Cook for 15 minutes.

Darne of grilled kingfish steaks

Serves 6

6 pieces of kingfish

2 lemons

1/2 tsp table salt

1/2 tsp pepper powder

1/2 tsp mustard

Cut 6pcs of king fish darne (steaks) and put in a basin, then marinate with salt, lemon juice, mustard and black pepper. Put in the over on moderate heat, after 15-20 minutes it is ready to be grilled.

The Dhow Restaurant

Built fifty years ago to trade spices between Tanga and Nungwi, the dhow of the title is now simply known by its Swahili name of *jahazi*. These days, however, the *jahazi* is a floating restaurant, ferrying just a few lucky passengers out to culinary heaven each evening in a small fishing boat.

The dhow's upper deck is a haven of peace, swaying gently with the tide and strewn with enormous floor cushions on which to recline gratefully while sipping a cocktail and watching the sun go down on the western horizon. After that, guests are invited downstairs to help themselves from a dazzlingly arrayed buffet of soups, fresh salads and side dishes presented in antique Swahili porcelain bowls and warmed where necessary over traditional earthenware braziers.

Lobster, prawns, calamari, octopus and many more are cooked to order over a sizzling brazier, heated with charcoal, which hangs over the side of the boat above the turquoise water. After dinner, satiated guests are served tiny brass cups of Arabic coffee to prevent them from falling asleep to the gentle movement of the sea.

Green mango and chicken salad scented with coriander

Serves 6

3 green mangoes (unripe)

1 head of green lettuce

1 chicken breast, cut julienne

1 bunch of coriander leaves

Juice of one lime

1 red onion

1 *pili pili* chilli

Cut the green mangos, red onion, lettuce and grilled chicken breast (cold) into strips (julienne). Add lime-juice, *pili pili* (chopped finely), pepper and salt and mix together in a big, elegant bowl. Chop fresh coriander and sprinkle over the salad.

Grilled seafood platter

Serves 6

6 calamari steaks

6 crayfish (medium size)

6 cigale de mer (rock lobster)

6 crabs (body or claws)

1kg prawns

1kg tuna fillet

1 house of garlic (crushed into a paste)

2 pili pili chillies

1 piece of ginger

Calamari Steak in ginger

Marinade the calamari steaks in the ginger paste (ginger, lime juice, olive oil) overnight. Grill the steaks for 5 minutes and cut them into strips. Filet the tuna and marinate in crushed garlic for 2-3 hours in the fridge Grill on the BBQ and serve medium rare.Use 2 chillies and chop them very finely. Add lime juice to the chilli and marinate the prawn kebabs in the mix. Grill on the BBQ for 5 minutes so they are still crunchy and not dry.

Add crayfish, rock lobster and crab to the grill. Choose an elegant platter and decorate the grilled seafood around the platter.

Okra ratatouille

Serves 6

7 aubergine

1 zucchini

1/2 kg green peppers

1/2 kg okra

7 big tomatoes

1/2 kg onions

1/2 crushed garlic house

Oregano

Salt and pepper

Olive oil

Fry onions and aubergine together in little olive oil for 10 minutes. Add green peppers and okra and leave simmering for another 5 minutes. Now add zucchini (cooks very fast), crushed garlic and lastly tomatoes. Season with oregano, salt and pepper and sprinkle with more olive oil before serving.

Salad of young spinach, avocado and prawns with a ginger-garlic dressing

Serves 6

1/2 kg young spinach, washed and plucked

2 avocados

1 head hard lettuce

1/2 kg of grilled king prawns

1 red onion

Ginger-garlic dressing

Crush 2 pieces of ginger into a ginger paste. Add garlic paste of 2 cloves of garlic to it and make liquid with lime juice. Finish off with salt and pepper to taste

Wash young spinach and mix with hard lettuce (cut julienne). Cut 1 onion into slices and mix into the salad. Open the avocados, remove the seed and cut into slices. Add avocado to the salad and top with grilled prawns. Serve the salad with the ginger-garlic dressing.

Tower Top Restaurant

An integral part of the skyline of Zanzibar, along with mosque minarets, Hindu temple towers, and church spires, the Tower Top restaurant of Emerson & Green Hotel is the second tallest building in Stone Town Zanzibar. Once the residence of Ismaili merchant Taria Thopan, one of the richest men in the Swahili Empire, the hotel has now been lovingly restored to its former glory. Each of the hotel's 10 rooms is a different shape and size – some small and tucked away under the eaves, some huge and imposing, with balconies looking down onto the cramped, hurrying streets of Stone Town below.

Just twenty-five diners at a time are allowed up to the converted Indian teahouse, now a restaurant, floating high above the rooftops of the capital. They remove their shoes to sit on Persian carpets and lean back against the silk cushions while the sun goes down behind the sultan's palace, muezzins wail the call to prayer and the triangular silhouettes of dhows slip past in the harbour. It is pure Arabian Nights fantasy, and Emerson has lost track of the number of couples who've got engaged while gazing across the brightly coloured turrets of the Hindu temple opposite.

Marinate the fish for 1 hour.

For the coconut crust, dredge each piece of fish in the flour, then dip in the egg mixture, and then roll in the grated coconut to cover evenly. Heat oil to 350F, and gently submerge into hot oil using a metal spatula until golden brown. If fish fillets are very thick you may want to finish cooking in a moderate oven until fish is cooked through. If using thinner pieces this will not be necessary.

For the sauce, put white wine, shallots, and garlic in a sauté pan, and reduce over medium heat by half. Add juice of bungo, and sugar and reduce over medium heat by half or until sauce becomes thick, almost like a concentrate. When the bungo mixture is reduced until quite thick, reduce heat to low, and whisk in the cubes of cold butter.

Make sure to use cold butter directly from the fridge, to the pan. Once the butter is whisked into the bungo reduction, the sauce is ready.

Coconut crusted fish with bungo sauce

Serves 4

For the coconut crust:

4 pieces of fish, preferably white, approx 200g each

400-500g grated coconut

1.5l vegetable oil

280g flour seasoned with salt and pepper

4 eggs, beaten

For the marinade:

2 cloves garlic, minced

2 tsp ginger, minced

2 tsp soy sauce

Juice of one orange

125ml of olive oil

For the sauce:

Juice of 4 bungo fruit

2 shallots, minced

1 clove of garlic

1 tbs sugar

250ml of white wine

110g butter, cut into cubes

Stuffed kingfish fillet with mango ginger sauce

Serves 4

4 fillets of kingfish or other white fish, 7 to 8 oz each

1 medium sized red onion

25g chopped fresh coriander

450g of crab or shrimp, cooked, and diced

250g pineapple, diced

4 eggs, beaten

140g flour, seasoned with salt and pepper

4 tbs oil for frying

Juice of 1/2 a lemon

2 tbs grated coconut

Using a paring knife, make an incision in the side of the fish without cutting all of the way through, just enough to make a cavity for the stuffing. Mix together in a bowl, the pineapple, onion, grated coconut, fresh coriander, cooked crab meat or shrimp, and juice of lemon. Stuff each piece of fish with stuffing mixture, dredge in flour.

Heat sauté pan, add oil. When oil is hot, place fish in pan and fry until golden brown. When fish is brown on both sides, finish cooking in a moderate oven until fish is just cooked - about 5 to 10 minutes depending on the size and thickness of the fillet.

For the sauce:

1 mango, chopped

1 tbs shallots, minced

1 tsp garlic, minced

1 tbs ginger

1 tsp soy sauce

Pinch of cumin

Pinch of cinnamon

1 tbs olive oil

Juice of 1/2 a lime

Heat olive oil, add shallots and fry lightly for 1 or 2 minutes. Add garlic and ginger, and cook for one more minute. Add cumin and cinnamon and stir well. Add chopped mango, lime juice, and soy sauce, and simmer for 8 to 10 minutes.

Passionfruit and calamari salad

Serves 6

1 kg cleaned calamari

5 passionfruit

1 red onion, diced

10g fresh coriander, chopped

Dressing:

2 tbs olive oil

1 tbs mustard

1 tbs garlic, minced

1 tbs ginger, minced

1 tbs soy sauce

Salt and pepper to taste

1 hot chilli pepper

Cook calamari tubes in boiling water until just cooked through. Cooking times depend on the thickness of the tubes. Drain and cool.

Halve the calamari bodies lengthwise and cut into very thin strips. Mix together all of the ingredients for dressing. Cut passion fruit in half and scoop out pulp and seeds. Add to the dressing. Add the calamari to the dressing along with the diced onion, and fresh coriander. Toss well and serve.

Zanzibar Serena Inn

Set in two historic seafront buildings, now masterfully restored to their former splendour, the Zanzibar Serena Inn, perched on the sea wall, exploits its grandstand view of the Indian Ocean from every angle and every room. The interiors, with their heavily carved wooden doors, thick Persian rugs and marble floors, echo the rich Arabian influences at work in Zanzibar.

Dining in the Serena's elegant dining room is a feast of variety - local seafood is a speciality but its preparation reflects the many cultural influences that arrived in Zanzibar with the various merchants who came to trade over the centuries. Naturally, local seafood is a speciality, the variety matched only by the imaginative use of Zanzibar's local herbs and spices used in its preparation.

The alfresco bar terrace affords magnificent views across the straits of Zanzibar and is the perfect spot to enjoy spectacular sunsets over the ocean and the continent of Africa beyond. For a post-dinner drink, the Serena's comfortable indoor bar, rather reminiscent of the inside of a luxury ship, evokes memories of old Zanzibar with porcelain plates and brass coffee pots lining the walls.

Kuku paka (chicken in coconut milk)

Serves 1

150g boneless skinless chicken cut into moderately big cubes

1 ml first press coconut milk

10g butter

1/2 tsp onion, garlic and ginger puree

1ml tomato concasse

Pinch of chopped coriander

1 hard boiled egg

A piece of steamed potato

1/4 tsp crushed cardamom

Brown the chicken pieces till golden brown. Meanwhile sautée onion, garlic and ginger puree with butter. Once cooked add crushed cardamon, tomato concasse, and coconut milk and bring it to boil. Then introduce the browned chicken into the mixture and let it simmer for three to four minutes and later add chopped coriander. Add the hardboiled egg and steamed potato and correct the seasoning to taste. Chopped chillies are optional. Serve with rice.

Chilli barbeque prawns

Serves 1

100g jumbo or king prawns in shell

Lemon juice

30g garlic, onion and ginger paste

1tbs soy sauce

1 chopped fresh chilli

Salt and pepper

For peri-peri sauce

30g garlic, onion and ginger paste

50g fresh tomatoes

100g tomato paste (optional)

Salt

Lemon juice

Prawn stock

Clean the prawns, split them and thread onto a skewer. Mix all other ingredients together and marinade the prawns in the fridge for an hour or two. Grill over medium heat. Meanwhile, sauté the sauce mixture and add deseeded tomatoes, and eventually the tomato paste and chillies. Add the stock and let the mixture cook. Once heated through, blend, strain and correct the seasoning. Serve the prawns with steamed rice or steamed potatoes and mixed vegetables. Serve the peri-peri sauce on the side.

Mocha crème brulée

Serves 4

5 egg yolks

2 whole eggs

5dcl double cream

80g sugar

1 tbs vanilla essence

Mix all the ingredients together and strain. Fill a suitable soufflé dish or casserole and poach in bain marie in a moderately hot oven. Once ready, sprinkle the top with brown sugar and place under moderate grill until golden brown.

Chocolate mousse

Serves 4

30g sugar

4 eggs, separated

50g sugar

Orange zest

80g unsalted butter

120g melted dark chocolate

150g pineapple

Beat the butter with the sugar until creamy. Add egg yolks in stages. Warm in a bain marie and add the melted chocolate at once as you stir carefully to avoid lumps. Add dissolved/melted dark chocolate and orange zest. Blend into the whipped cream. Finally whisk the egg white to a meringue and fold in carefully. Fill into desired moulds - teacups, dessert dishes etc - and top with pineapple caramelized with sugar.

Around Stone Town

A visit to the smaller coastal villages around Stone Town provides an interesting insight into the history of Zanzibar. Bububu, for example, a lively village just a few miles north of town, holds the remains of the once-famous Zanzibar Railway, built in the early 20th century to run from the Old Fort on the seafront for six miles along the coast.

Just south of Bububu, at Mtoni, tucked in among the palm trees, lie the remains of Beit-al-Mtoni – the 'house by the river'. Built during the nineteenth century reign of Sultan Said, the first and greatest of the Omani sultans in Zanzibar, Beit-al-Mtoni was for several years home to the Sultan's queen as well as his many concubines. Over a thousand people lived in splendour next to the sea, with tame gazelles and peacocks wandered between the opulent bathhouses and around the courtyard.

But the Omani sultans were not alone in building imposing reminders of their reign in Zanzibar. During the nineteenth century the English Bishop Steere oversaw the establishment of a colony for freed slaves on the coast at Mbweni, just south of Stone Town. He was assisted by Miss Caroline Thackeray, one of the indomitable spinsters so beloved of the British Empire, who founded a school for former slave girls, now in ruins, among lush tropical gardens.

Imani Beach Villa

Set right at the edge of the Indian Ocean in the historic village of Bububu, the Imani is a enchanting little boutique hotel in the midst of a tropical garden laden with palms, banana trees, fragrant flowering plants, and passion fruit. Imani has its own private beach, equipped with large beach umbrellas, sun shades and *chaise longues*, an ideal spot for having a drink while admiring a magnificent view of the sea, dotted with traditional fishing boats, or watching herons fly across each evening to one of the small islands nearby where they spend the night. The beach at Imani is a lively place, always buzzing during the day with women in their colourful kangas gathering shellfish, or young Africans practicing yoga or martial arts along the ocean shore.

The Imani Beach Villa restaurant is designed in traditional Moorish style, with low tables made out of coconut wood and decorated with veils and colourful cushions. Billowing silks and rich Persian rugs make the Imani restaurant one of the most sumptuous in Zanzibar, with the exotic charm of the legendary *1001 Nights*. Every morning, breakfast includes fresh fruit straight from the lush fruit trees that surround the villa.

Tambi za naza
Taglioni with coconut sauce

Serves 4

1/2 kg tagliolini (linguine)

1/4 teaspoon nutmeg powder

Coconut

Salt

Chilli pepper powder

Boil tagliolini in three litres salted water for 5 minutes.
Take tagliolini out of hot water and stir-fry with coconut
sauce for 5 min.

Coconut Sauce:

Mix one cup of shredded coconut mix with nutmeg, a
pinch of chilli powder and salt

Mixed seafood salad

Serves 4

1/4 kg jumbo prawns

1/4 kg calamari

1/4 kg octopus

1 medium-sized fish

1 carrot

1 fresh tomato

1/4 kg cabbage

1 cucumber

Mayonnaise

Tomato sauce

Chilli sauce

Boil prawns, octopus, calamari and fish until soft; let cool
and cut into small pieces. Prepare a mixed salad with
cabbage, carrot, cucumber, and tomato and put in a
bowl. Place salad on plate and top it with the boiled
seafood. Serve with cocktail sauce - to make it, mix mayonnaise, tomato sauce and chilli sauce.

Coconut crusted tuna

Serves 4

1/2 kg fresh tuna

50g wheat flour

2 eggs

1 coconut

1/2 l cooking oil

1/2 tsp curry powder

Black pepper

Salt

Divide the fish into four portions. Mix wheat flour with
salt, black pepper, and curry powder. Mix egg whites in
bowl. Heat cooking oil. Roll fish in flour, egg whites, and
coconut sauce; fry in hot cooking oil. Pour over coconut
sauce, food is ready to serve.

Coconut Sauce:

Mix one cup of shredded coconut mix with nutmeg, a
pinch of chili powder and salt.

Fish ravioli with almond sauce

1/4 kg wheat flour

400g kingfish

Cheddar cheese

4 eggs

1 tbs butter

2 tsp almond powder

250g fresh tomatoes

Black pepper

Pinch salt

Mix flour with egg until well blended. Roll the dough as flat as a paper napkin. Boil kingfish and salt to taste, let cool, take out all bones. Mix kingfish with black pepper, cheddar cheese then divide into four portions. Put the mixture of kingfish with black pepper and cheddar cheese on each portion on the napkin shape and fold, using egg whites as a sticky binding; press with fork to close, optional automatic fork decoration. Bring salted water to a boil; then boil ravioli for 3 minutes.

Sauce for ravioli :

Put butter and almonds in frying pan; stir while heating, and after 2 minutes mix in ravioli.

Chop tomatoes and top the ravioli on each plate.

Mangapwani Seafood Grill

Visitors to Mangapwani, the Zanzibar Serena Inn's beach restaurant, are offered a fresh seafood barbeque – lobster, giant prawns, crab claws, octopus and more – cooked to perfection over traditional charcoal braziers by an expert team of chefs. The atmosphere is informal and friendly, and the restaurant comprises a series of traditional *makuti* bandas, all set into a lush hillside overlooking the beach. Polished wooden tables and chairs of cheerful blue canvas, are tucked into a small cliff among the trees.

As well as swimming on the pleasant, sandy Mangapwani beach, guests who arrive for lunch can also enjoy fishing, snorkelling, kayaking, catamaran rides and other activities at the well-equipped watersports centre.

Close by, a sombre reminder of Zanzibar's cruel past, lies a slave cave, a hollow cavern in the ground where up until the nineteenth century hapless slaves, captured on the mainland of Africa and brought to Zanzibar by sailing dhow to be sold on to the plantations of the middle East, were stored before transit.

Meanwhile, sautée the onion paste, add the seeded dates, tamarind juice, stock and coconut milk and bring it to the boil. Blend the mixture and strain, correct the seasoning. The claws are best served with rice or potatoes and fresh market vegetables, with the date sauce on the side.

Grilled rock lobster

600-700g lobster
Juice of half a lemon
Salt and pepper
30g unsalted butter
10g ginger, garlic and onion paste

Marinate the rock lobster using the lemon juice, salt, pepper and paste. Let it stand for 30 minutes in the fridge and place on grill on moderate heat. Make sure that the grill marks appear nicely for presentation purposes. Meanwhile, clarify the unsalted butter and add lemon juice, correct the seasoning. Once cooked, the lobster can be served with steamed rice, buttered parsley potatoes and mixed vegetables. Garlic butter sauce should be presented on the side with a lemon wedge.

Crab claws

100-140g crab claws, shelled half way
2tbs lemon juice
Salt and pepper
30g garlic, onion and ginger paste
200g sieved white breadcrumbs
1tbs dark mustard seeds
20g wheat flour
2 whole eggs, beaten
1l vegetable oil

Date sauce

30g seeded dates
250ml tamarind juice
250ml pressed coconut milk
250ml concentrated crab stock
30g garlic, onion and ginger paste

Season the crab claws with lemon juice, salt, pepper and paste. Pass it through wheat flour, beaten eggs and eventually white bread crumbs and mustard seeds. Deep fry the claws in moderately hot oil until cooked, ensuring that they acquire a golden brown colour.

Tiger prawns tandoori

5 or 6 tiger prawns, threaded on a skewer

For marinade:

1 tsp yoghurt

1 tbs turmeric

2 tbs tandoori spices

Juice of 1 lemon

Let the prawns stand in the marinade for five minutes, put on the plate and bake in the oven at a moderate heat. When ready, remove the prawns and put aside while you put the juice back onto the heat together with the marinade, and reduce it by 1/3. Correct the seasoning and sieve. Arrange the prawn skewer on a platter and pour the sauce over the top. Any extra sauce can be served on the side, along with rice or buttered potatoes and a lemon wedge.

Seafood platter

70g lobster

60g prawns

40g fish fillet

40g calamari - threaded onto skewer

30g crab claws

For marinade: garlic, onion, ginger and lemon juice

For sauce:

Coconut milk

Fish stock

Ginger, garlic and onion paste

First marinade all the seafood and fish for several hours. Then bake them in the oven. Meanwhile sauté the garlic paste, add stock and add pressed coconut milk. Boil the mixture, sieve, and correct the seasoning. Once the seafood is ready, arrange on the plate and fill ramekin with sauce for serving on the side. Goes well with potatoes or rice.

Mbweni Ruins Hotel

Seven kilometres south of Stone Town on the coast at Mbweni lies a flourishing botanical garden containing over 650 plant species as well as a fine variety of birds and butterflies. Neat paths meander around the garden, set next to a mangrove-fringed beach and skirting around the famous Mbweni Ruins. The ruins are all that remains today of St Mary's School for Girls, built by the redoubtable Miss Caroline Thackeray in 1871 to help rebuild the lives of the young girls whose families were killed or scattered by the slave trade. At St Mary's, young girls were trained as teachers or nurses, or taught useful skills such as basket weaving, cookery or needlework to allow them to live independently. Torchlit dinners are now held in the ruins of the chapel, among typical Swahili architecture.

One of the paths through the garden leads to the Raintree Restaurant, where, among resolutely Swahili surroundings – wooden chests, intricately carved doors and comfortable four poster beds – sundowners of Pimms, gin and tonic or Swahili fruit punch are served before a sumptuous meal of traditionally prepared Zanzibari seafood. Desserts are based on the fresh, succulent fruit that grows in abundance on the garden's many mango, banana, passion fruit and bongo trees.

40g garden peas

40g green pepper

40g spring onions

40g potatoes

30g cashew nuts

12g sultanas

2 bunch coriander

1 onion

35g biriani masala

1 clove garlic

100ml plain yoghurt

200ml vegetable stock

Saffron

Ginger

Cinnamon sticks

Onion for garnish

Salt and pepper

Kiamati

Serves 1

100g wheat flour

10g yeast

50g sugar

250ml corn oil

35ml water

40ml coconut milk

25g cardamom

Local honey

Mixed spices

Mix together the flour, yeast, cardamom and coconut milk. Leave to prove for 10 minutes. Fry in hot oil, drain and dip in local spiced honey.

Unguja biriani: local Zanzibar biriani curry

Serves 1

250g long grain rice

40g carrots

40g cauliflower

Slice the onions, ginger and garlic and fry until a rich golden brown. Chop all the vegetables, the Biriani masala and the coriander, stir fry with the onions for 10 minutes and then add the vegetable stock and simmer for 10 minutes. Cook the rice and drain. Soak the saffron in water, rinse and drain the rice. Add the cashew nuts, cinnamon sticks and sultanas. Drain the water off the saffron and mix together with the rice.

Whole baked sea perch in green banana and coconut sauce

Serves 1

6 green bananas

400ml coconut milk

1 sea perch whole

65ml lime juice

50g onion

50g tomato

Garlic and ginger

Salt and pepper

Peal the banana and slice it in half. Place the banana in boiling water for 10-15 minutes, drain and rinse in cold water. Place the sea perch in the oven and bake for 20 minutes. Slice the onion, tomato, garlic, ginger and gently fry. Add the coconut milk and simmer for 10-15 minutes. Season to taste, place the sea perch on a plate and serve with the sauce.

Kamba kwa nazi: king prawns tossed in a rich coconut sauce

Serves 1

150g king prawns

200ml coconut milk

5g garlic

15g onions

15g fresh tomato

1tsp turmeric powder

1/2 bunch coriander leaves

Salt and pepper

20ml corn oil

Peel the king prawns and fry in corn oil in a heavy bottomed pan. Add garlic, ginger, onions and sauté together. Add in coconut milk, turmeric, salt and pepper and bring to the boil. Turn down the heat and simmer for 10-15 minutes. Serve with steamed rice and traditional flat bread.

Mtoni Marine
Restaurant

Set on a stretch of beach just two kilometres from Stone Town, Mtoni Marine restaurant is one of the true fine dining experiences of Zanzibar. On tables set on the sandy beach or amid soft lighting under the palm-thatch roof, guests can sample an eclectic à la carte menu of imaginatively presented dishes, based on African ingredients but cooked according to European methods. The creators of all this are Waldemar Mueggenburg and Stephanie Schoetz, a South African/Dutch couple who trained together in Germany before meeting again ten years later and moving to Zanzibar to take over Mtoni Marine, fusing their love of the spices of Zanzibar with Waldemar's classical continental training.

Waldemar revels in sourcing the freshest and purest local ingredients, using a selected group of suppliers, and finding new methods of using the abundant fruit and seafood available in Zanzibar to create demanding, surprising, and above all delicious recipes. Only the best produce from local farms, and seafood selected daily by the chef, is used to create Mtoni Marine's exciting fusion of classic continental cuisine and the aromatic spices of Zanzibar.

Soft music from the regular local bands that are invited to play at Mtoni Marine restaurant, impeccable service and the pretty beach location all combine with the unforgettable food to make this one of Zanzibar's most popular and upmarket dining spots.

Grilled tuna fillet, skewered on lemongrass, enriched with a cumin flavoured lobster buerre blanc

Serves 1

180g tuna fillet

1 lemongrass stalk

Olive oil

Salt and ground pepper

Rub the filet in with olive oil. Season, and spike the filet with the lemongrass stalk. Seal the filet on a hot grill and allow to rest before baking it pink in the oven.

Cumin lobster buerre blanc

200ml lobster bisque soup

Pinch of whole cumin

1 chopped red onion

Olive oil

200g cubed butter

Sauté the onions and the cumin in the olive oil so as to release the full flavour of the cumin. Add the lobster soup and allow to boil for 30 min. The soup will get thicker, like a sauce, and take on the flavour of the cumin. Strain the sauce so as to remove the cumin and the onions and

bring back to boil. Remove from heat, add the butter and blend with a hand mixer. Do not boil the sauce again as this will cause the butter to separate from the lobster sauce.

Marinated tomatoes

18 plum tomatoes cut lengthwise in half

2 red onions, chopped

4 garlic cloves, chopped

1 bunch parsley, chopped

1 tbs sugar

100ml olive oil

Salt and pepper

Aluminium foil

Place the half tomatoes in a deep tray with the skin side down. Sprinkle over the tomatoes the onions, garlic, parsley, sugar, salt & pepper and the olive oil. Cover the tray with aluminium foil. Place the tray in a low heat oven (100C). Bake slowly until the tomatoes start going soft.

Serve with mashed potatoes. Place the mash in the centre of the plate. Bury two or three marinated tomatoes in the mash. Place the tuna steak on the tomatoes and pour the sauce around the plate. Garnish with a poached egg and coriander leaves.

Salad of oven braised leg and thigh of chicken and marinated red cabbage, with a mango-tomato salsa

Serves 1

Leg and thigh of 1 chicken
Enough olive oil to cover the leg when placed in a pot
Crushed garlic cloves
Sliced whole fresh ginger
Crushed peppercorns
Sliced onions
Sugar and salt

Place all ingredients into a high pot and make sure the legs are sunk in oil. Place on a low heat with a lid and allow the legs to braise at a low temperature in the oil. This process should take about two hours so the meat gets very soft, nearly falling off the bone, and can absorb all the flavours from the oil. Remove from the oil, cool down on a rack so all excess oil can drip off. When needed, replace in the oven until the skin is golden brown and crispy.

Salad of marinated red cabbage

Red cabbage sliced very finely
Red wine
Orange juice
Honey
Lime juice
Olive oil
Crushed spices: cloves, cardamom, chilli, cinnamon
Salt and pepper

Add all ingredients into a flat tray and toss to mix well. Spread the mixed cabbage evenly over the tray and cover with cling film. Place in cold room over night to allow the cabbage to "bleed", marinade and soften. Before removing the cabbage from the tray, toss once more and remove, leaving the juices behind.

Tomato and Mango salsa

1 mango, peeled and cut into small cubes
3 tomatoes, peeled and cut into small cubes
Olive oil
Lime juice
Salt and pepper
Chopped parsley

Mix the mango, tomato and parsley together. Marinade with lime, oil, salt and pepper. Place the hot baked chicken leg on a bed of cold marinated red cabbage, drizzle the salsa around the plate. Garnish with potato crisps and a bunch of coriander leaves.

The East

Unlike the more groomed beaches of the north and west, the beach that runs down the east of Zanzibar island is wide and rugged. It is one of the few places in Zanzibar where a sense of infinite space and freedom is conjured up by the contemplation of a wide horizon – the vast blueness of the Indian Ocean on one side, and the sweeping line of palms curving off into the distance on the other. The tide goes out for miles here; leaving behind ladies bent like colourful driftwood over their seaweed farms, rock pools fringed with delicate green weed and studded with starfish, whitened chunks of whalebone – a beachcomber's paradise.

The eastern side of Zanzibar is thought to have been settled by Persian immigrants before western part of the island and the present day capital, Zanzibar Town, were developed. Dotted along this coast, in the villages of Paje and Bwejuu, are the remains of ancient mausoleums and mosques, almost completely ruined and nestling in obscurity among the scrubby vegetation on the village outskirts.

The East Coast villages are built from coral rag, held together with limestone cement and then whitewashed, sheltered from the rain by palm-thatch roofs. The stunning stretch of beach known as Kiwengwa is famous for its luxury hotels, which provide unsurpassed views of the ocean panorama from shady courtyards, romantic dining rooms and elegantly decorated bedrooms.

Bluebay Beach Resort

Bluebay Beach Resort is situated on a beautiful 25 acre beachside site, with its bedroom cottages located on rising ground overlooking verdant gardens, a lagoon swimming pool, more than 1,000 beautiful palm trees, and a sparkling white beach. The hotel's reception area invokes the interior of a wealthy Arab house of the era of the Sultans, with its cool marble floors, elegant archways and tinkling fountain. All the spaces at Bluebay are decorated using traditional Zanzibari furniture, both antique and modern, including hand-carved chests inlaid with brass, beaten pewter pots and Indian-style darkwood writing bureaus inlaid with tiles.

The hotel's Makuti Restaurant, with locally-carved wooden furniture and bright, checked tablecloths, enjoys magnificent views over the swimming pool to the ocean beyond. The Beach Bar and Restaurant, as the name implies, is situated on the very edge of the sea and is an ideal place for guests to sip cold drinks or to enjoy seafood specialties or pizzas prepared in an authentic wood fired oven, all served in an informal setting with toes in the sand and a magnificent thatched roof to provide shade from the hot tropical sun.

Chicken in lemon sauce

Serves 1

250g oven ready chicken.
2 or 3 lemons
Salt
White pepper
1/2 glass white wine

Remove any string from the chicken and spread the bird out without actually cutting it apart. Pour over the the juice of 2-3 lemons, making sure that the juice moistens every part of the chicken. Season with salt and pepper and leave overnight to marinate in the juices. Next day put the chicken in an oven-proof pan with the remaining juices. Do not add any butter or oil. Preheat the oven to 325- 350F and place the bird in the oven. Roast for about 1 hour, basting two or three times during the cooking with spoonfuls of the dry white wine. Serve with fresh seasonal vegetables.

Thai noodles

Serves 2

1 pack spaghetti or wheat noodles
1/2 kg Chinese mushrooms
1/2kg okra (lady's fingers)
3 kg carrots
1 leek
2 baby marrows
2 sticks celery
4 tbs soy sauce
3 tbs oyster sauce
Coriander leaves

Slice vegetables finely and bring to the boil in a hot pan. Cover for ten minutes. Add 1/2 litre water, soy sauce, oyster sauce, and spaghetti. Simmer for 5 minutes. Serve.

Avocado salad and shrimps with Italian dressing

Serves 2

2 avocados
100g raw shrimp
1/2 an onion
1/2 litre olive oil
6 tbs lemon juice
Tomato to garnish
Salt

Remove the shells and boil the shrimp in salted water with onion, lemon and salt for 2 minutes. When they are ready, put them in iced water. Slice avocado and spread into a circle.
Place the shrimps next to the avocado on the plate and prepare the dressing:
Shake olive oil and lemon juice with salt and pepper together and cover the avocado and shrimps. Serve chilled.

Cold cut Mediterranean menu

Serves 6

1 kg beef fillet, slightly frozen
Juice of 3 lemons
1/2 l olive oil
Sliced parmiggiano cheese
2 sticks sliced celery

Arrange the sliced beef on a plate. Top with: parmiggiano cheese, olive oil, celery and lemon juice.

Grilled red snapper in garlic sauce with sliced tomato

Serves 6

6 red snapper steaks
2 tbs white flour
1/2 l garlic olive oil
Sliced tomato
Green pesto
Olive oil
Market vegetables eg carrots, potatoes, runner beans
Salt and pepper

Dust fish with flour and pan fry in hot oil, add braised vegetables, boiled rice. Garnish with sliced tomato, drizzled with pesto.

Breezes Beach Club

The beautiful Breezes Beach Club in Bwejuu certainly lives up to its name. Fresh, cooling winds blow constantly through the variety of innovatively designed spaces that make up this effortlessly elegant hotel. The chief characteristic of Breezes – apart from its superb location – is the aesthetic flair and attention to detail that have been brought to the interior design. Use of fabrics is particularly strong – burnt orange silks are tied to traditional beds in the so-called Swahili Room, leopard print sofas complement the dark wood of the bar, and the delicately fluttering pink curtains of the lightest chiffon form the walls of the breezy Upepo Lounge.

Dining at Breezes carries with it the same focus on the finer details. Alongside traditional Zanzibari seafood, various other world cuisines, from India to the Middle East, are also represented on an imaginative and eclectic menu. Guests can also choose a variety of locations in which to sample Breezes' cuisine – the main dining room, with pale pink tablecloths and wrought iron candlesticks, the Makuti a la carte restaurant, built on stilts overlooking the beach, romantically candlelit by silver-beaded table lamps, or, more intimate still, the Tides – private dining for two right at the edge of the water.

Chilled vegetable soup with coriander & chilli and garlic bread croutons

Serves 4

200g finely chopped onions

300g cucumbers

200g green peppers

200g fresh tomatoes

25cl tomato juice

2 tsp red wine vinegar

2 tsp lemon juice

3 tbs olive oil

5 tsp water

Fresh red chilli chopped (according to taste)

Salt and pepper to taste

Roughly chop all the vegetables and pass briefly through a food processor (vegetables should not be pureed). Add the vinegar, lemon juice, olive oil, tomato juice and water and mix well. Season with salt and pepper and add the chopped fresh chilli to taste. Chill for at least half an hour before serving with garlic bread croutons and a touch of cream.

Spiced crab cakes with chilli oil

Serves 4

200g finely chopped onions

300g crab meat

3 spring onions chopped

2 small pieces of ginger grated

1 tsp coriander chopped

2 tsp mayonnaise

1 fresh chilli chopped

Salt and pepper to taste

Breadcrumbs

Cooking oil

Chilli oil

Chopped fresh chillies

Salt and pepper

Red chilli powder

Olive oil

Blend all the ingredients together to make a paste (the mixture should not be too stiff). Form the mixture into individual "cakes" and refrigerate for half an hour so that they set. Cover the crab cakes in breadcrumbs and then fry in hot oil for about 2-3 minutes. For the chilli oil, soak the fresh chillies in the olive oil for at least two hours adding salt, pepper and chilli powder to taste.

Breezes crab in ginger served with saffron steamed rice

Serves 4

4 whole crabs

80g finely chopped onions

60g chopped garlic

100g of finely grated ginger

40g butter

3 tsp soy sauce

1 tsp vinegar

2 tsp lemon juice

Cook the crabs in salt water. Remove the claws, crack them slightly and keep separately. Remove the remaining crabmeat from the shell. Clean the shell thoroughly and keep for serving. Melt the butter in a large pan, add the onions, garlic, ginger and allow to sizzle for about 2 minutes. Add the crabmeat, crab claws and soy sauce and vinegar to taste. Lower the heat and allow it to simmer for a few minutes. Carefully place the crabmeat back in the shell and serve together with the claws and saffron rice.

Flambéed pineapple craquelin served with coconut ice cream

Serves 4

8 slices of pineapple (centre removed)

40g butter

2 tbs brandy

2 tsp cinnamon

1 lemon

4 tbs sugar

1dl orange juice

Cut the pineapple slices into cubes. Gently melt the butter in a large pan and place the pineapple cubes in the pan. Cook gently for a few minutes. In a small bowl mix the lemon juice, orange juice, sugar and cinnamon. Pour the mixture into the pan and allow it to cook for about two minutes. Finally add the brandy and flambé the pineapple. Lower the heat and leave it to cook for another four minutes. Serve hot with a scoop of coconut ice cream.

Karafuu Hotel

Karafuu means 'clove' in Swahili. Cloves are Zanzibar's most important spice, having arrived in Zanzibar in 1818. They were recognised as an important source of income by Zanzibar's first Sultan, Seyyid Said, who encouraged the planting of clove trees on his lands. Zanzibar rose to become the world's top clove producer, during the second half of the nineteenth century providing 90 per cent of the world's clove supply. Today the fragrant, aromatic scent of cloves is one of the enduring memories of any visit to Zanzibar, with the tiny green buds being painstakingly hand-picked before being spread out in the sun on bamboo mats to dry.

Karafuu Hotel, as befits its name, was built in harmony with the environment from local materials and using local building traditions – dried coconut palm leaves for the roof, coral rock and limestone cement for the walls. Inside Karafuu, the interior design is based around a number of very elegant antique and reproduction pieces from the era of the sultans, including wall clocks and *chaises longues*, complemented by imaginative use of fabrics such as silk and satin. Dining at Karafuu provides guests with a wide choice of experiences, with no less than four restaurants within the hotel itself.

Fresh Jozani Forest mushrooms on toast

Serves 1

100g Anchor butter

1/2 tsp garlic

Pepper and salt

Parsley

200g mushrooms

2 slices bread

Fry the butter in the pan, add the garlic, pepper and salt, add the mushrooms, let it fry for a few minutes, then add the slices of bread, let it brown a little.

Put on a plate, put the mushrooms on the 2 slices of toast and decorate with parsley.

Noodles with fresh Jozani mushrooms

Serves 1

50ml olive oil

1 pack wheat noodles

200g mushrooms

Parsley

Pepper and salt

Heat olive oil in a wok, add the mushrooms and let them fry for a few minutes, add pepper and salt, noodles, and parsley, let it all fry for a few minutes. Toss ingredients together and serve.

King prawns with fresh ginger and mango

Serves 1

200g king prawns

50ml soy sauce

1 mango

Olive oil

1/2 glass white wine

Fresh ginger

Pepper and salt

Put the olive oil in the wok, fry the king prawns till they become nicely red, add the soy sauce, fresh ginger, mangoes, pepper and salt and half a glass of white wine, let it all fry for a few minutes. Serve with spiced rice.

Mapenzi Beach Club

Mapenzi Beach Club is that rare thing – a large beach resort with character. Its single storey rooms, set amidst lush tropical gardens, give Mapenzi Beach Club a relaxed, rather charming character. The enormous makuti roof – reportedly the largest in East Africa – hides a variety of shady, tastefully decorated relaxation areas, from the cool terrace restaurant to the little tea platform perched high above the rest. Here guests can recline on cushions or on a traditional Swahili bed, watching the wind in the palm trees or playing cards, board games or traditional Zanzibari pastimes such as *bao*.

Dining at Mapenzi Beach Club is nothing if not lavish – the hotel is famous for its sumptuous lunch and dinner buffets, tables groaning with a feast of Italian specialities – pasta, pizza, Osso Bucco and a variety of salads - alongside more traditional Zanzibari fare such as grilled fish, sweet potatoes or coconut rice. For those who prefer to feast on seafood, straight from the ocean and prepared to order, Mapenzi's Suli Suli grill chefs are happy to oblige. To work up an appetite for all this, guests are able to interrupt their sojourn stretched out on the beach with activities such as tennis, archery, or watersports.

Cigale de Mer with squid ink sauce and tagliatelle

Serves 4

4 shoe lobsters (cigale de mer)

2 litres Court-Bouillon

8 shallots

20g butter

40ml Noilly Prat

800ml fish stock

120gr butter

Ink from 4 small sepia squid

Salt

White pepper.

200g fresh tagliatelle

4 tbs vegetable oil,

4 diced peeled tomatoes

4 tsp chopped parsley

Bring Court-Bouillon to the boil. Add the shoe lobster and boil for 3-4 minutes. Remove the tail meat from the shell. Chop the shallots and simmer in 20g butter, add Noilly Prat and fish stock and reduce to 1/4. Add the butter in small pieces to bind the sauce. Colour the sauce with the ink. Add salt and white pepper. Keep the sauce warm. Cook the fresh tagliatelle "al dente". Heat the oil in a frying pan, sautée the tails and add the diced tomato and the chopped parsley. Divide the sauce into 4 plates, add the tagliatelle and the tails and top with the tomato dice.

Zanzibari seafood gumbo

Serves 4

600g lady's fingers (okra pods)

100g carrots

150g spring onions

100g celery

2 tomatoes

4 tbs vegetable oil

3 chillis

Garlic paste

Juice of 2 limes

1/2 litre chicken bouillon

250g shrimps or prawns

1 rock lobster tail (approx 250gr)

Crab claws (approx 500gr, can be replaced with same quantity of local shellfish)

Pinch salt

2 tbs freshly chopped herbs (basil, thyme, parsley, coriander)

Prepare okra pods by taking off the stem and cutting them into pieces. Boil them for 3 to 4 minutes in salted water. Clean and chop (small) carrots, celery and spring onions. Heat the oil in a big clay pot and add the chiselled chilli (without the seeds) and the garlic paste, and sweat gently. Add the chopped vegetables and stew for 4-5 minutes.

Add the okra pods and the tomato cut into cubes (without skin and seeds) and simmer for another 4-5 minutes. Add whole shrimps/prawns, crab claws and the lobster tail cut into pieces, cover the pot and simmer at low heat for about 15 minutes.

Banana tarte tatin

Serves 4

150g puff pastry

75g white sugar

2tbs water

30g butter

1kg bananas

50g soft light brown sugar

60g butter

Juice of 1 lemon

250ml fresh cream

Roll puff pastry to a 25cm circle, prick well with a fork. Combine white sugar and water in a small pan and stir it into a golden caramel. Turn off the heat and blend with 30g butter. Pour into a 23cm round fixed bottom cake tin.

Peel bananas, and cut in half vertically and arrange them tightly packed (round side down) onto the caramel. Sprinkle a little lemon juice and the soft light brown sugar on top and dot with the remaining butter. Place the disc of puff pastry over the bananas, tucking the edges to hide the fruits. Bake for 35-45 minutes in a preheated oven at 190° until the pastry is puffed and golden. Leave to cool in the tin for 30 minutes before turning out and serving with whipped cream.

Sultan Palace Hotel

In 1828, the flagship of Sultan Seyyid Said, the ruler of the tiny, rocky kingdom of Oman at the mouth of the Persian Gulf, docked in the harbour of Zanzibar. Used to the dusty, dry and hostile environment of Oman, Said was delighted by the cool, green island of Zanzibar, with its abundant fresh water and agreeable climate. In 1840 he moved his court permanently from Oman to Zanzibar, and his descendents formed the royal house of Zanzibar for the next 123 years.

Sultan Palace hotel, inspired by the elegance of the era of the Sultans, is situated next to a turquoise lagoon on a beautiful white sand beach on the south-east coast of the island. The fifteen enormous Nautilus shell shaped cottages, each named after a flower, are individually designed and elegantly furnished with local antique furniture including carved Omani doors and Zanzibari beds.

The restaurant, with its splendid wooden terraces facing the ocean, welcomes guests into a bright parqueted lounge. The Arabic terrace is the place to relax and enjoy aromatic spiced coffee or tea whilst gentle winds blow from the ocean. Meals are served in the local beach bandas during lunch and candlelit romantic dinners on the terrace offer fresh seafood and various other local specialities.

Lobster catalana

Serves 1-2

1 cooked lobster

1 sliced red onion

2 potatoes (boiled & cubed)

5g black pepper, crushed

25ml red wine vinegar

25ml olive oil

Salt to taste

Remove the flesh from the lobster and cut into bite size pieces. Mix with cubed potatoes, onion, dress with vinegar, olive oil, pepper and salt. Place in fridge to cool down. Present on starter plate, dish the mixture into the lobster tails. Shell and garnish with lemon and fresh herbs.

Curried kole kole fish

Serves 4

800g Fillet kole kole or white fish

60g red onion (sliced)

60g green pepper (julienne)

60g leeks (julienne)

200g tomato (cubed)

60g baby marrow (julienne)

60g green beans (french slice)

100g curry powder

50g cardamom

20g cinnamon sticks

10g chillies (chopped)

30g garlic (chopped)

Salt & pepper to taste

Sauté all vegetables, add spices and fry to release flavour. Add tomato and allow to simmer. Place the fish fillet on top and cover, allow fish to poach with steam of sauce. Season to taste. Serve on a bed of rice, covered with curry sauce.

Beef stroganoff

Serves 4

200g beef fillet julienne

40g dliced red onion

40g green pepper (cleaned & julienned)

5g black pepper crushed

40g mushrooms (sliced)

25ml olive oil

15ml soy sauce

10m cream

Salt to taste

Sauté the fillet & pepper julienne, mushrooms and sliced onions with olive oil in a hot pan. Add soy sauce, salt and pepper to taste. Add cream, simmer for a minute. Serve on fried rice.

Profiteroles

Serves 2

Choux paste:

250ml water

125g flour

100g butter (unsalted)

4 eggs

Whipped cream

Dark chocolate, melted

Bring water to the boil. Add butter and flour whilst stirring with a wooden spoon, remove from heat when mixture stops to stick to the side of the pan. Let the mixture cool. Add eggs and mix well. Pipe mixture into rosettes and bake in oven till golden brown. Remove from oven and allow to cool. Pipe whisked cream into the centre and serve with chocolate sauce.

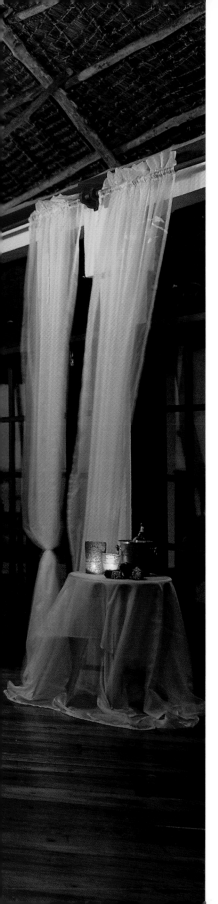

The Palms

The Palms is a small, elegant beach retreat just outside the village of Bwejuu. Romantic, Arabian Nights style private beach villas, each decorated with the silks and colours of the east, look out onto the vast white sweep of the beach. Colours are predominantly rich browns and creams, with smooth honey-coloured marble floors and carved wooden beds.

The Palms concept is laid back and luxurious - breakfast is served by a private butler in the comfort of each villa, followed by a morning spent lazing by the dark blue lagoon pool. Exotic tropical lunches are taken on the pool terrace, and for afternoons on the beach, each villa is provided with a private banda on the sand.

Dinner is served in the elegant central plantation house, indoors or on the wide colonial style verandah that faces the sea. For a nightcap, guests can lie back in their private jacuzzis and listen to the sounds of the Indian Ocean lapping at the shore just yards away.

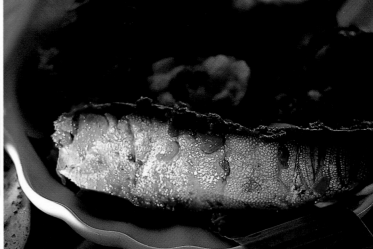

Smoked sailfish & rosti potato stacks served with horseradish & lemongrass cream

Serves 2

1 tbs horseradish cream

Finely chopped fresh lemongrass (can be substituted with dill)

2dl cream

Salt & pepper to taste

Lime zest

5 large potatoes

1 egg (beaten lightly)

4 tbs flour

1 clove garlic, minced

Oil and butter for frying

100g smoked sailfish thinly sliced (you can substitute smoked salmon)

Rosti potatoes & sailfish stacks

Roughly grate four large potatoes and drain the water completely with a kitchen towel. In a bowl mix one egg, the grated potatoes, garlic, flour, salt & pepper to taste. In a pan add the oil and butter and bring to high heat. Place the potato mixture on the hot pan flattening to form small round pancakes. Fry until crispy golden brown on both sides. Slice the smoked sailfish into thin slices and season lightly with salt & pepper.

Horseradish and lemongrass cream

Finely chop the lemongrass and place into a bowl. Add salt, pepper, whipped cream, lime zest and the horse-radish and mix all the ingredients into a smooth mixture. Leave to cool.

Place the potato stacks on the plate and add a table-spoon of the horseradish cream. Place the sliced sailfish on the potato rosti and add another layer.

Indian Ocean bouillabaisse served with garlic baguette and chili aioli

Serves 2

4 tbs olive oil

4 tbs butter

3 cloves garlic, minced

2 large onions finely chopped

4 cigale de mer (shoe lobster)

2 large lobster tails (cut into pieces)

6 king prawns with shell (heads removed)

5 ripe tomatoes finely chopped

1dl tomato puree

4 tbs freshly chopped coriander

1 fresh red chili (finely chopped and seeds removed)

1dl fish stock

1dl water

2dl dry white wine

Baguette bread, grilled in the oven with some garlic/parsley butter

1 fresh red chilli (finely chopped and seeds removed)

8 tbs mayonnaise

2 cloves garlic (finely chopped)

Salt & pepper to taste

In a large pot add the olive oil and butter and bring to a medium heat.

Add the garlic and chopped onions and fry until golden brown. Carefully add the cigale de mer, lobster tails and king prawns. Mix carefully and place the lid on the pot and leave to cook for about 3 minutes. Remove all the seafood and place on the side. Add the chopped tomatoes, puree, coriander and fresh chopped red chili. Add the stock, water and white wine and cook for a few minutes. Place the seafood back in the pot and cover leaving it to simmer over low heat for about 20 minutes. For the aioli, mix the mayonnaise, finely chopped garlic and freshly red chili and add salt & pepper to taste.

Serve this dish in deep soup bowls with a tablespoon of aioli in the center of the plate and with grilled garlic baguette on the side.

Red snapper wrapped in banana leaf served with spiced butter and a potato & pumpkin bake

Serves 2

2 pieces of red snapper fillet
2 tbs lime juice
Salt & pepper
1 tsp cumin seeds
1/2 fresh red chili (finely chopped)
2 tbs chopped fresh coriander

1 tsp freshly grated ginger
2 tbs olive oil
2 large sweet potatoes (very thinly sliced)
2 large regular potatoes (very thinly sliced)
Salt & pepper
3 tbs cream
1 tsp cayenne pepper
100 g salted butter
2 tbs chopped parsley
2 cloves finely chopped garlic
2 tsp paprika
1 tsp cumin powder

Blanch the potato slices in boiling water for about one minute. Layer the sweet potato and pumpkin in a baking tray, adding salt & pepper to each layer. Mix the cream and cayenne pepper and pour over the top. Bake in the oven until cooked.

Season the fish fillets with salt, pepper and sear the fillet in a hot pan for about one minute on each side. Remove from the pan and add the lime juice, cumin seeds, chili, ginger and coriander. Wrap each of the fillets individually in banana leaves (can be substituted with greaseproof paper or foil). Before sealing, add the olive oil. Place on a baking tray and allow to cook for about 15 minutes. Remove the leaves and serve with the potato and pumpkin bake and spiced butter.

The North

The large villages of Nungwi and Matemwe at the north end of the island are traditionally the hubs of Zanzibar's boat-building industry. Dotted along their picture-postcard perfect beaches are the skeletons of giant dhows, propped up on struts as they are planed, hammered and tempered with fire to make them seaworthy enough to be launched, with much pomp, on the first of many trading or fishing journeys across the glittering turquoise ocean. Today, however, the dhow-building economy of the north has been superseded by the tourist industry – dozens of hotels and guesthouses have sprung up on the headland around the village, ranging in quality from luxury to budget.

There is certainly no question that the coastline around Nungwi and Matemwe seems almost to have been created to fulfil the dreams of even the most extravagant sun-seeker. The sand is white, powdery and cool even in the hottest sun; coral cliffs overhanging the beach provide welcome pools of black shade, and the water is blue, translucent and inviting. As sun sinks slowly below the horizon, palm trees, sand, sea and sky are bathed in a mellow orange glow, alongside the inert bodies of visitors who came here for a few days and remained for months…

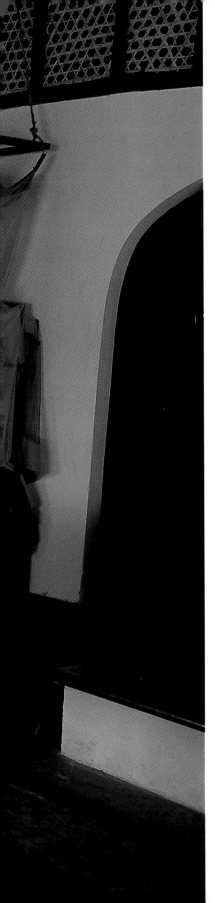

Matemwe Bungalows

After 12 years of loving care, the cool, green garden of Matemwe Bungalows forms a small oasis overlooking the ocean in the otherwise dry scrubland of the northeast coast of Zanzibar. Matemwe Bungalows' 15 bandas are ecologically friendly, using solar power for electricity and hot water, and are built entirely from local materials. Guests can enjoy the comings and goings of the local *ngalawa* fishing fleet from the comfort of each private terrace or from the pleasant, shady restaurant. Early morning tea and coffee, accompanied by home-made biscuits, is served on the veranda. Dinner is fresh seafood, straight from the ocean, cooked and served with an oriental touch – wooden chopsticks, bamboo mats, and tiny, spicy bowls of vegetables.

The gardens and exterior spaces of Matemwe Bungalows are decorated with entertaining and sometimes startling marine artefacts - including the skeleton of a ten-metre sperm whale, which beached itself on the nearby reef. The hotel's diving operation, Dhow Divers, is one of the few dive centres that still use the traditionally made local wooden dhows for diving and snorkelling operations. A school, teacher's accommodation and vegetable garden have all been set up in co-operation with the local village, using donations from hotel guests.

Rock oysters on the beach

Serves 2

12 rock oysters

Lemon wedges

Tabasco

Scrub grit and sand off the oyster shells. Wrap one hand in a cloth and hold the oyster in it. With the flatter part of the oyster on top, take an oyster knife and gently prise the oyster open at the hinge. Cut the ligament and lift of the top shell. Place them on some ice and ready to serve with a squeeze of lemon and a drop of tabasco.

Pepper crab

Serves 2

2 crabs cooked, cleaned and quartered with meat remaining in the shell

1 tbs garlic

2 tbs onion

2 tsp oyster sauce

2 tsp dark soy sauce

1 tsp sugar

2 tsp roughly ground pepper

1 ladle oil for frying

Fry the garlic and onion in the oil for 2 mins in a pot. Add the oyster sauce and soy sauce and mix in. Add the sugar and pepper and let sizzle in the pan, mixing well. Add the crab pieces stir to cover with sauce. Cover with lid and let stand for 5 mins.

Ready to serve alone or with steamed rice and Chinese vegetables.

Zanzibass

Serves 2

100g icing sugar

200g digestive biscuit crumbs

100g dark cooking chocolate

200g ground nuts dried

Egg white from 2 eggs

50g grated coconut

Place icing sugar, crumbs, nuts in a bowl and mix together. Melt chocolate and add grated coconut then pour into the bowl with the other mixed ingredients and mix well. Beat the egg whites until peaking and then fold into mixture. Put into a tray of 8cm circle and 3cm height and sprinkle with coconut crumbs and refrigerate for 5 hours.

Kairamashikio

Serves 2

250g flour

100ml coconut milk

1 tsp sugar

Place flour, sugar, and coconut milk in a bowl, mix well into smooth dough and cover for 10mins. Divide dough into separate balls and roll out until very thin. Mould into shape requested. Heat cooking oil and drop individual shapes and fry until golden.

Serve with a kisheti on top and drizzle honey over the top.

Kisheti biscuits

Serves 2

100ml coconut milk

50g grated coconut

250g white flour

150g sugar

10g yeast

500g cooking oil

Place the flour, coconut milk, yeast and 50 grams of sugar in a bowl and mix together until a smooth dough, leave covered for 10 minutes. Roll out into long strings and twist into a figure of 8 pattern. Wait for 8 minutes before deep frying until golden. Heat rest of sugar with a little water in a small pan and simmer until syrup thickness. Coat with the syrup, roll in coconut gratings and serve.

Ras Nungwi Beach Hotel

Discerning visitors to the opulently perfect beaches of the Nungwi peninsular stay at Ras Nungwi Beach Hotel, the village's smartest establishment - although words like 'smart' and 'upmarket' convey impressions of gilt taps and gold jewellery, which is not what Ras Nungwi is about at all. It's much more informal, with the waiters who serve dinner being quite happy to sit down for a game of cards afterwards!

There are so many cushions at Ras Nungwi - piled along the top of low walls, beckoning invitingly from the wood and string sofas, nestling in hammocks suspended from date palms - that it's a wonder any guest can resist their siren softness and actually remain vertical long enough to stagger from beach to pool to table. The central sitting and dining areas are linked by a giant palm thatch roof that protects everything from the occasional tropical rainstorm, blurring the distinction between inside and outside so that even sitting in front of an elegantly-set dinner table, visitors never really lose that barefoot, sand-between-the-toes feeling.

The colours and textures of the ocean are everywhere at Ras Nungwi - turquoise and dark blue glass tiles of exactly the same hue as the sea on either side of the reef float in the infinity swimming pool and merge seamlessly with the sky. Newly-caught kingfish, seasoned with green chilli and basil, is guided skilfully straight from line to pan, and onto the plate at lunchtime.

Barbequed kingfish steaks with couscous, dates, basil and ground almonds with a green chilli gazpacho sauce

Serves 6

6 Kingfish fillets

Juice of 2 limes

3 tbs olive oil

Salt

1 tsp cumin

1 clove crushed garlic

Place all ingredients into a large bowl and mix well. Add kingfish fillets and refrigerate for several hours. In a hot pan with olive oil, fry fish until light brown.

For the sauce

4 diced tomatoes

1 seeded and finely diced cucumber

1 finely diced green pepper

1 finely diced onion

2 cloves crushed garlic

1/2 cup breadcrumbs

6 tbs olive oil

2 tbs red wine vinegar

1 tsp sugar

Salt and pepper

3 finely sliced green chillies

Mix all ingredients together in a bowl and refrigerate for 30 minutes before serving.

Couscous

600g couscous

600ml boiling fish stock

3-4 finely diced dates

Chopped basil

150g ground almonds

Salt

Place couscous into a large mixing bowl. Add fish stock and salt. Set aside and let cool. Add all other ingredients and break up with a fork.

Seared tuna with a cucumber, ginger and orange salad with a fresh coriander and pimento dressing

Serves 6

6 x 3 mm x 3 mm steaks fresh tuna

3 seeded and cubed cucumbers

2 cm ginger (grated)

2 skinned and sliced oranges

100ml premium soy sauce

1 shaved leek

Olive oil

Marinate tuna in soy for about 30 minutes. Toss cucumber, ginger, spring onions and orange in olive oil. Arrange in the centre of the plate. Quickly sear tuna in a hot flat pan and place on top of your salad.

Dressing

1 small bunch fresh, chopped coriander

50g cleaned, drained and fine diced pimentos

250ml olive oil

2 tbs white vinegar

2 tbs spoons lime juice

1 tbs sugar

Salt

Zest of 1 lime

Blend all except pimentos. Add pimentos and use to dress the plate.

Lala salama lobster with garlic, coconut milk, mango and white wine

Serves 2

1 x 500g lobster

3 tbs flour

2 tbs spoons butter

250g grated cheese

1/2 glass white wine

1 crushed garlic

1/2 small mango, cubed

240ml coconut milk

60ml lobster stock

Remove lobster meat from shells. Boil and drain (keep stock). Cube meat. Fry butter, garlic, salt and pepper. Make white sauce with lobster stock, flour and white wine add little cheese and remove from heat. Add mango & coconut milk. Mix all together with meat, fill lobster shell, cover with remaining cheese and grill. Serve with brown rice seasoned with ground cardamom seeds.

Zanzibar Beach Resort

The centerpiece of the cheerful Zanzibar Beach Resort is the huge, convivial Fat Harry's Bar, sheltered from the blustery sea winds by a huge makuti roof. The bar itself is carved from marble and sunk into the floor, allowing guests plenty of room for propping it up during the long, lazy afternoons, or admiring the panoramic view of sea and sky from under the eaves.

The whole of the Zanzibar Beach Resort has a carefree, watersports-orientated atmosphere, with a fully equipped dive centre and a range of boards, sails, boats and skis big enough to satisfy the most demanding adrenalin junkie. After a hard day on the ocean, guests can relax in the dining area, which is two storeys high, decorated with carved wooden tables and canvas easy chairs, and brightened up with funky Tinga Tinga style cushions the same deep blue as the swimming pool.

At regular intervals, a seafood barbequeue is held on the beach to celebrate, with the day's big game fishing catch having pride of place on the menu. Huge piled-up platters of seafood are decorated extravagantly with flowers, banana leaves and herbs. Food is cooked to traditional seafood recipes, with a touch of the Orient added by the judicious use of eastern spices and flavourings.

Lobster tails in mango sauce

Serves 4

4 lobster tails

2 sticks lemon grass

2 large mangoes

1 glass white wine

6 mint leaves (chopped)

Boil lobster tails until shell goes pinky/red, approximately 10 minutes, set aside. Peel mango and blend, then strain, add juice to a pot and bring to the boil. Add wine and simmer for 2 minutes. Add the chopped mint and lemon grass. Pour over lobster and serve on a bed of tagliatelle.

Thai calamari coconut curry with basmati rice

Serves 4

1 kg calamari, cut into goujons

2 cloves garlic

1 stem ginger

2 stems lemon grass

4 green chillies

2 tbs basil (chopped)

2 bunches coriander

1 tbs corn flour

1/2 tsp nutmeg

4 red onions (chopped)

1/2 tsp cardamon

1/4 kg green beans

1 tbs fish sauce

700ml coconut milk

Garnish: 1 bunch of coriander

Add all ingredients except the coconut milk, calamari and beans to a wok. Fry for 3 minutes then add the calamari and cook for a further 3 minutes. Add the coconut milk and simmer until it thickens. Garnish with chopped coriander and serve with basmati rice.

Seared tuna fish steak and king prawns with sweet tomato and lime coulis

Serves 4

4 tuna steaks (approximately 40mm thick)

8 king prawns

Coarse salt and pepper

4 limes

For the coulis:

1kg plum tomatoes (cubed)

1/4 kg demara sauce

1 red chilli (chopped fine)

1 tbs fish sauce

Juice of 4 limes

1/2 tsp cinnamon

1/2 tsp nutmeg

2 tbs sweet soy sauce

1 tbs corn flour

1 bunch of coriander (chopped)

120ml water

Coulis

This should be made first and can be warmed when ready to serve. Add all the ingredients to a pan and simmer for 10 minutes. Just prior to serving add coriander.

Fish: Rub salt and pepper into the steaks. Squeeze limes over the prawns. Cook prawns on a hot griddle for 7 minutes, put aside. At this point sear steaks for 2 minutes each side, remember middle of steaks should be pink. Pour over coulis and serve.

Chilled devilled crab

Serves 4

4 crab bodies

2 tuna fillets

2 cloves garlic

1 stem ginger

1 tsp paprika

4 limes

Knob of butter

Mayonnaise

Boil crab bodies until deep red in colour, approximately 7 minutes, allow to chill. Open crab bodies and remove all white meat, put to one side. Pan fry tuna fillets in butter, lime juice, garlic and ginger, allow to chill. Mix crabmeat, tuna, paprika and enough mayonnaise to bind. Divide mixture into the 4 crab body tops, chill for two hours and serve.

Islands

A round Zanzibar's principal islands of Unguja and Pemba, an archipelago of smaller islands lie studded like jewels in the crystal blue of the Indian Ocean. Some are merely sandbanks, visible only at low tide, while some are uninhabited save for seabirds, snakes or bats. Some have religious or historical significance - Misali Island, to the west of Pemba, is reputed to have been used as a hideout by the notorious pirate Captain Kidd, who is even said to have buried treasure here. Locals believe the island is holy, having been used by the prophet Hidara as a prayer mat.

But a few are more substantial, with coral reefs, dense rainforests and tempting sandy beaches, just waiting for a modern-day Robinson Crusoe to be washed up. These islands are a truly untouched vision of paradise: turtles lay their eggs on the white sand beaches, dolphins swim and play in the surrounding waters, shy antelope hide in the forest and shoals of brightly coloured fish flit across the reef.

On Zanzibar's private islands, visitors are made to feel like honoured guests, with luxurious accommodation, subtly designed architecture and most importantly of all, the feeling of utter privacy and seclusion that only comes from having the beach to oneself.

Chapwani Private Island

Chapwani is a magical little private island, surrounded by small coves with white sandy beaches and coral reefs, which lies just outside Stone Town. Just five bandas line the water's edge, decorated with colourful African prints and furnished with local antiques and four poster beds. The restaurant, housed in an airy, relaxing dining room with open walls, provides a satisfying and beautifully presented blend of Oriental, African and Italian cuisine based around fresh local fruits and seafood.

The thick tropical vegetation of baobabs, palm trees and passion fruits that covers Chapwani harbours a rich variety of wildlife including a herd of miniature antelopes known as dik diks, as well as several interesting bird species and the rare and endangered coconut crab.

Along the South West Coast of the island runs the sea wall protecting the small but fascinating British seamen's graveyard. The white, marble graves through tell the stories of the hapless crewmen of various British ships in the last two centuries who lost their lives in battles with Arab dhows during the slave wars, accidents at sea and the sinking of HMS Pegasus, the first shot to be fired in the First World War.

Gazpacho

Serves 6

2kg red tomatoes, peeled and quartered

2 small cucumbers, seeded and chopped

2 medium red onions, chopped

30ml balsamic vinegar

60ml olive oil

1 tsp sugar

2 tsp Tabasco sauce - or less according to taste

1 tsp freshly ground black pepper

850 ml tomato juice

2 tsp parsley, finely chopped

Croutons

900g unsliced white bread

60g butter

2 tbs olive oil

Blend or process tomatoes, cucumbers, onions, garlic, vinegar, oil, sugar, parsley, sauce and pepper until roughly chopped. Combine in a large bowl with tomato juice. Cover and refrigerate for 3 hours or overnight. Serve cold, topped with croutons.

For croutons: Trim crusts from bread, cut into 3 cm cubes. Heat half the butter and oil in a large pan, add half the break, cook, stirring, until lightly browned and crisp. Drain on absorbent paper. Repeat with remaining ingredients.

Smoked snapper with straw potatoes and lime coriander dressing

Serves 6

6 fillets red snapper

Salt & freshly ground black pepper

Pinch tumeric

150ml fresh lime juice

1 bunch fresh coriander

2 tbs olive oil

Mix salt, pepper and tumeric with 50 mls lime juice and pour over the fish fillets. Mix well so that all fish surfaces are covered. Place in the fridge for 3 hours or more. Clean coriander and remove stalks. Chop finely and mix well with 100 mls lime juice and olive oil. Place in fridge until serving.

Soak smoked chips in water for 10 minutes, then drain and squeeze out excess moisture. Prepare an indirect fire in a kettle braai and when coals are hot, sprinkle with smoke chips. Place fillets along centre of grill, cover and cook for 20 minutes. Remove, cool and serve with coriander and lime dip.

Embroidered fish

Serves 6

1 whole red snapper or similar - about 2 kg.

3 leeks, trimmed and finely sliced into matchstick lengths

2 carrots, cleaned and finely sliced into matchstick lengths

1 large green pepper, seeded and shredded

2 cloves garlic, crushed

5cm piece fresh ginger, peeled and sliced

50ml soy sauce

Lemon slices and green olives for garnish

Clean the fish and make five or six cuts on one side. Place garlic and ginger in the fish cavity and sprinkle inside with soy sauce. Stuff each of the cuts with alternate types of prepared vegetables. Wrap fish in foil and place on a rack over a large pan of simmering water. Cover tightly and steam for about 20 minutes or until fish is tender. To serve, line a serving plate with salad leave and carefully place fish on top. Garnish with lemon slices and olives. Serve with steamed or fried rice.

Coconut bananas with caramel sauce

Serves 4

6 firm bananas

Plain flour

2 eggs lightly beaten

80g grated coconut

2 tbs dry breadcrumbs

Oil for deep frying

Caramel sauce:

300g brown sugar

200g castor sugar

300ml water

200ml coconut milk

1 dessertspoon corn flour

1 tbs water, extra

20g butter

Cut bananas in half lengthwise, toss in flour, shake off excess and dip bananas in eggs, then in combined coconut and breadcrumbs. Just before serving, deep fry bananas in hot oil until lightly browned, drain on absorbent paper. Serve hot bananas with caramel sauce.

Caramel Sauce

Combine sugars and water in pan, stir over head without boiling, until sugars are dissolved. Bring to the boil and boil uncovered for about 8 minutes, or until golden brown. Stir in coconut milk and blended corn flour and extra water. Stir until sauce thickens slightly, remove from heat, add butter and stir until melted.

Chumbe Island Coral Park

Six kilometres south of Stone Town, surrounded by pristine coral reef, Chumbe Island is one of the world's newest and most successful eco-tourism projects. In 1994, the reef surrounding Chumbe Island was made Tanzania's first Marine National Park. The island itself, covered with lush mangrove forest, is a designated forest reserve. Chumbe Island Coral Park won the British Airways Tourism for Tomorrow Award in 1999, in recognition of seven years' conservation work carried out in co-operation with local fishermen, now retrained as marine wardens.

In addition to seven state-of-the-art eco-bungalows for visitors, Chumbe Island contains a lighthouse, a ruined mosque, and the lighthouse keeper's house, now converted into a spectacular education centre and restaurant. Under a magnificent makuti roof, sometimes likened to Sydney Opera House, friendly waiters bring out a seemingly endless string of steaming pottery dishes filled to the brim with healthy, organic dishes made from local ingredients.

Visitors can come for the day to snorkel over the incredible coral reef, which contains over 370 species of fish, turtles and dolphins. Guided walks are also available through the island's coral rag forest, interspersed with tidal pools and huge baobab trees, which supports a unique flora and wildlife population including the rare -- and enormous -- coconut crab.

Cold fish salad

Serves 6

6 pieces of good fish

4 onions

1 clove garlic

3 avocados

1/2 tsp salt

2 lemons (or lime)

3 cucumbers

2 green chillis

Spices (pepper, ginger, paprika to taste)

2 big tbs olive oil

2 large tomatoes

Clean and fillet the fish and put together with lemon juice, salt and pepper, chilli and ginger and a little water in a container and leave in the fridge for 15 minutes. Put the oil in a pan and fry the roughly chopped onions and garlic until soft. Remove the fish from the fridge and add to the onions and garlic and cook on a low heat until the fish is cooked right through. Leave the fish to cool and slice the tomatoes, cucumber and avocado and arrange on dish. When fish is chilled, place between the salad and serve.

Serve with an assortment of cold salads, including cold rice salad, carrot and orange salad and fresh green salad.

Chilli beef with Zanzibar spinach and coconut rice

Serves 4

1kg minced meat

2 onions

1 clove garlic

2 fresh tomatoes

1 small tin tomato paste

1 piece ginger

1/2 tsp salt

Water

1 fresh chilli

Boil the meat in water with the onions, salt, garlic and ginger on a low heat for 20 minutes. Add the tomato paste, fresh tomato and chilli and continue to boil over a low heat. Add chilli powder to taste.

Zanzibar spinach

2 bunches spinach

2 coconuts

1/2 tsp salt

2 onions (chopped finely)

1 garlic (chopped finely)

2 fresh tomatoes (chopped finely)

Water

Clean the spinach and roughly chop. Boil it with a very small amount of water until it has reduced by half. Slowly add the chopped tomato, onion and garlic to the spinach, stirring all of the time. Grate the coconuts and rinse the meat (of the coconut) with fresh water keeping the residue. Once it has settled a little, scoop the creamy substance off the top and add slowly to the spinach, stirring all of the time. Cook to your preferred consistency. After a couple of minutes the spinach will be ready to serve.

Serve with freshly baked Naan bread and coconut rice.

Chumbe Chicken Curry

Serves 6

2 chickens

4 onions - chopped

1 inch piece of ginger

1 pint chicken stock

Mixed spices

1 cup lemon juice

2 tbs cooking oil

1/2 tsp salt

4 cloves garlic

Curry powder to taste

Boil the chicken in water with mixed spices and half of the ginger until it is cooked through. Strain the chicken taking care to keep the stock for cooking later. Bone the chicken.

Heat the oil in a pan and add the onions and garlic and the remaining ginger. Cook the onion until tender. Slowly stir in the curry **powder** so that it becomes a paste. Gradually mix in the **chicken** stock, lemon juice

and then finally add the chicken and bring to the boil again, ensuring that the chicken is heated through.

For a spicier curry, add chilli powder. Serve on a bed of steamed rice with side dishes of tomatos, hard boiled eggs, cucumber, green pepper, all chopped finely, coconut and chutney.

Mnemba Island

Mnemba, an Arabic word meaning octopus head, is a rather unromantic title for what must surely be one of the world's most romantic hotels. Mnemba Island Lodge consists of a cluster of ten ensuite cottages, spread out in perfect seclusion along a spectacular white sand beach. The style of Mnemba is very much understated luxury combined with rustic simplicity – the bedrooms are built of local wood, topped with airy roofs of makuti palm thatch in the traditional manner of coastal dwellings in Zanzibar. Beds are vast, mosquito net swathed affairs, carved by local artisans, and each cottage has its own private sitting area and sunlounger. A straw sunhat and a bundle of cotton kikois are piled up on the bed, and a palm-thatch walkway connects each cottage with its turquoise coloured bathroom, complete with beauty products in delicate glass bottles.

Dinner is freshly caught fish and seafood cooked on the beach in a barbeque pit, and tables and chairs are set out on the sand at twilight, surrounded by hurricane lamps and flares. The innovative fusion cuisine is based on local produce, and accompanied by chilled white wine in chunky glasses. The dining concept at Mnemba is much like the overall design – elegant simplicity in stunning surroundings.

Fruit and nut biscotti

Serves 6

500g plain flour

500g sugar

1 tbs baking powder

5 eggs, lightly beaten

100g sultanas

100g dried mango, diced

100g chopped dates

100g pistachio nuts

100g almonds

100g cashew nuts

3 limes (grate the zest and discard the fruit)

Preheat oven to 180 degrees celsius. Mix flour, sugar and baking powder in a large bowl. Add half of the beaten eggs and mix well, then add half again and mix again. Add the last quarter until your dough takes shape, but isn't too sticky. Add the fruits, nuts and lime zest. Divide the dough and roll into sausages about 3cm in diameter. Place on baking paper on baking trays. Wet your hands and lightly flatten the sausages then bake until golden brown. Remove from oven and leave to cool and firm up (about 10 mins). Reduce the temperature on the oven to 140C. Cut the Biscotti with a serrated knife on an angle into 5-10 mm pieces and lay on baking trays. Return to oven and cook for 10 mins on each side or until pale golden in colour. Cool on a cake rack and store in airtight jars. Will store for up to 2 months.

Chargrilled wahoo wrapped in banana leaves with coriander chutney

Serves 4

4 Wahoo fillets

To make the Chutney;

Large bunch of coriander

3-4 sprigs mint

2 green chillies

2.5 cm fresh ginger

5 cloves garlic

75g freshly grated coconut (or creamed)

4-6 tbs wine vinegar

1/2 tsp salt

1 tsp sugar

Blend chillies, ginger, garlic and coconut in a food processor. Add the coriander, mint, vinegar, salt and sugar. Blend well. Heat banana leaves on grill so they don't split. Cover both sides of each Wahoo fillet with chutney. Wrap in banana leaf and grill for approx 3 minutes each side on a hot fire.

Chilled curried apple soup with dried apple rings

Serves 6-8

1 Granny Smith apple

15g butter

1 onion, chopped

1 tbs mild curry powder

1kg Granny Smith apples, peeled cored and chopped

1l chicken stock

175ml single cream

Juice of 1-2 lemons

Salt and pepper

Preheat the oven to 100 degrees celsius. Thinly slice the single apple, the thinner the better. Place the apple pieces on a wire rack set over a baking tray. Place in the oven to dry for about 30 - 60 minutes, or until the apple slices are completely dry, turning once during cooking. Remove the apple slices from the wire rack and cool on greaseproof paper. To make the soup, in a saucepan, melt the butter and sweat the onion. Add the curry powder and cook for 1 minute. Add the chopped apples, chicken stock and some salt and pepper. Bring the mixture to the boil and simmer covered for about 1 hour.. Liquidise the soup, then strain it through a sieve and leave to cool. Add the single cream and fresh lemon juice to taste, then adjust the seasoning as necessary. Place the soup in the refrigerator to chill, then serve in chilled bowls with the dried apple slices as a garnish.

Red Cabbage and noodle Salad

Serves 2

White and/or red cabbage, sliced very finely
50g slivered almonds, roasted
50g sesame seeds, roasted
60g sunflower seeds, roasted
1 pack thambi noodles

Boil and drain noodles and toss in a little oil, so as not to stick, then spread very thinly on a slightly oiled baking tray and roasted in the oven till golden. Roast nuts and seeds individually, first the almonds, then sunflower seeds, then the sesame seeds, in a heavy based saucepan on the stove (easier to prevent burning), mix all together and cool.

Dressing

120ml sunflower oil
100g brown sugar
120ml white wine vinegar
1 tbs soya sauce
1 vegetable stock cube, blended with a little boiling water.
Mix in a jar with lid, shake well (lasts in the refrigerator for 2 weeks or more). Place the shredded cabbage in a serving dish, toss with a little of the dressing 1/2 hour before serving, mix in the nuts and roasted noodles and toss, top again with extra nuts and noodles just before serving. The nut mix , noodle, and dressing mix will last in the refrigerator for weeks, make sure the nut and noodle mix are in air tight sealed containers.

Fattoush salad

Serves 10

8 cucumbers, peeled completely, seeded and quartered
10 tomatoes, seeded and sliced
8 red onions, very thinly sliced
8 green peppers, chopped small
4 bunches parsley, roughly chopped
4 bunches mint, roughly chopped
3 lettuce heads, torn small
3 bunches rocket (or as much as the garden allows)

Dressing

1/2 cup lime juice
6 garlic cloves, minced
1 cup olive oil
1 bunch coriander leaves and stems, cleaned

Blend all ingredients and toss with the dressing just before serving. Serve with crackerbread.

Passion fruit and galliano sorbet

Serves 2

240ml orange juice
240ml syrup
120ml Galliano
480ml strained passionfruit juice

Whisk together the passionfruit juice and the syrup. Add the orange juice. Freeze and when nearly frozen then add the Galliano. Freeze in short glasses. Serve with a half slice of orange.

Coffee ice cream

Serves 10

1l milk
20 egg yolks
225g sugar
2 tins (170grms) sterilized cream
3 tbs instant coffee (or more to taste)

Boil milk then add egg yolk and stir over low heat until thick. Mix in sugar, and then slowly add cream and coffee. Remove from heat and allow cooling. When cool put in ice cream machine until ready. Serve in chilled glasses with fruit & nut biscotti.

Pemba

Smaller than its larger neighbour Unguja, as well as being lusher and hillier, Pemba is, comparatively speaking, scarcely visited by tourists, and its many stunning beaches, fringed by mangroves, are unspoiled and otherworldly. In the earlier years of the twentieth century, Pemba was famous the world over for the power of its sorcerers and magicians, with devotees of the black arts coming from as far away as Haiti to be initiated into the rites of Pemban witchdoctors. By all accounts, Pemba is still a centre of witchcraft today, but visitors will be unlikely to see any hint of the occult. Instead Pemba offers the chance to float across spectacular coral reefs, laze on untouched beaches and explore the winding hills and dense vegetation – including several pieces of pristine rainforest - of the interior.

Visitors to Pemba may be surprised to find that bullfighting is a popular local sport, supposedly imported by Portuguese invaders in the 17th century. The Pemban version, however, simply involves testing the skill of the bull in a series of bold moves by the matador, after which the bull is loaded with flowers and praise, and paraded around the village.

Fundu Lagoon

I n a secluded islet in the south of Pemba lies Fundu Lagoon, Pemba's most luxurious hotel. Created by a team that includes international fashion designer Ellis Flyte, Fundu Lagoon is an oasis of calm, sophisticated style in a stunning location. Just 20 individual rooms are dotted along the mangrove forest that lines the white sand beach. Each is designed like a 1920s safari tent, with cool, crisp linens, a hanging canvas wardrobe and a wooden writing desk. Each tent opens onto a private verandah with easy chairs, and steps leading down onto a personal sunlounger on the beach.

Fundu Lagoon's public spaces are likewise cool and elegant, but more contemporary in feel, with polished wooden floors, earthenware vases and billowing canvas drapes. Guest dine on international fusion cuisine either in the restaurant, surrounded by jungle and looking out across the sea, or on the 'New England' style jetty bar. This is a simple space of wooden decking and green canvas, with rope stools, old-fashioned ship's lanterns and even a whole canoe, suspended above the bar. In the evening, as the sun sets across the peaceful ocean, dolphins sometimes swim into the bay and around the jetty, their backs glistening in the golden sunset light.

Smoked wahoo with roasted beetroot and horseradish
Serves 2

250g wahoo (kingfish fillet)

200g sliced beetroot

2tsp lime juice

4tbs olive oil

Salt and pepper

Marinate wahoo with lime juice, salt and pepper and leave for 30 minutes. Grease the olive oil on a baking tray and arrange the beetroot on to the tray with some salt and pepper seasoning. Put the tray in a preheated oven for about 45 minutes. Put the wahoo in a smoker for about 1 to 1 1/2 hours and smoke until cooked. Put cut banana leaves on a plate and decorate with roasted beetroot, smoked wahoo and horseradish.

Wambaa poached snapper
Serves 4

4 red snapper fillets

1 tbs grated ginger

1-2 chopped red chillies

1 tbs chopped garlic

1 tsp turmeric

3 lime leaves

1 bunch lemon grass

500 ml strong coconut milk

Salt and pepper

Mix coconut milk, ginger, chilli, turmeric, lime leaves and lemon grass together and leave to infuse for 2 hours. Place snapper fillets in the coconut milk and leave to infuse for another hour. Take fillets out and pour mixture into a sauce pan and simmer for 5 minutes, add salt and pepper to taste. Serve with coconut rice, pumpkin or cassava leaves (alternative-spinach) and garnish with lemongrass.

Fundu's lobster fritters with lime aioli
Serves 4

8 small sized lobster tails

500ml cooking oil

2 tbs lime juice, salt and pepper

250g wheat flour

150ml water

2 eggs

1 tsp baking powder

200g mayonnaise

1 tsp chopped garlic, lime juice to taste

Peel lobster shell (put aside for decoration) and gently pull out dark vein from the meat, starting from the head. Cut each tail into 4 small pieces and marinate with lime juice, salt and pepper for about 30 minutes. Mix mayonnaise, garlic and lime juice together and whip into a light aioli. Mix flour, baking powder, eggs and water into a thick batter. Put oil in a frying pan and put onto a stove. Toss the lobster shell under salamander until changed to pink colour. Arrange shells on a plate and put fried lobster pieces back into it. Drizzle some aioli over it and garnish with a lemon wedge.

Pemban goat curry

Serves 4

1kg of leg or shoulder goat
3 cloves of chopped garlic
80 ml olive oil
2 tsp ground cumin
1 tsp ground ginger
1 tsp ground turmeric
1 tsp ground paprika
1/2 tsp ground cinamon
1/2 tsp ground cardamom
2 thinly sliced onions
600ml beef stock
50g raisins
250ml coconut milk
2 fresh chopped red chillies
1 tin tomato paste (70g)
Salt and pepper

Cut goat meat into small pieces, put in a bowl and add 2 tbs of olive oil and the garlic and leave to marinate for 30 minutes. Put remaining olive oil into a frying pan and add cumin, ginger, turmeric, paprika, cinnamon, cardamon and fry for 2 minutes. Add onions and fry until brown. Add goat meat and tomato paste and stir frequently for another 5 minutes. Add beef stock and reduce heat and simmer for 1 1/2 hrs. Add coconut milk, raisins, chilli, salt and pepper and cook for further 30 minutes. Serve with naan bread, rice and mango chutney.

Pemba Afloat

Pemba Afloat comprises three magnificent 20 metre yachts that are permanently moored in the tranquil waters of the Njao Inlet, at the north western tip of Pemba. The boats are reached after a bumpy and colourful drive through the rural villages and hills, valleys and paddy fields that characterise Pemba's countryside.

Pemba Afloat's yachts offer accommodation for a maximum of 8 guests, an exclusive group comprised mostly of diving enthusiasts who come to sample Pemba's famously pristine reefs, which offer a diversity of diving conditions, coral and marine organisms unequalled elsewhere on the East African coast.

Non-divers, however, find plenty to while away the long lazy days - breakfast on a white sand beach followed by a morning's snorkelling, or perhaps a wander through the unspoiled pathways of the Ngezi Forest, an untouched indigenous forest protected since the days of the sultans, ending up with a picnic on a pristine coral beach and a swim in Pemba's crystal clear emerald sea.

At dusk, a sumptuous dinner comprising freshly caught fish and island fruit and vegetables is laid on the aft deck, as carmine bee-eaters dart and swoop around the mast and broad winged Pemba flying foxes flap heavily across the waters. Sometimes the children from Mkia ya Ngombe, the nearest village, collect fresh mussels and oysters and row out to the yachts in their dugout canoes to sell them.

Banana and date cake

Serves 6

16 dates with stones removed

5 ripe bananas, mashed

2 eggs

225g sugar

3 tbs butter

225g flour

2 tsp baking powder

1 tsp bicarbonate of soda dissolved in warm water

Cream the butter and sugar together, beat in the eggs. Add mashed bananas, dates and bicarb. Sieve flour together with baking powder and gently stir into banana mixture. Spoon into large bread tin and cook gently for at least an hour. If you can, leave and refrigerate.

Mirella's baked mango

Serves 1

Take a mango cheek, score and sprinkle with cinnamon and brown sugar. Put under a very hot grill until the sugar caramalises. Serve with fresh coconut cream.

Ringapau ya Pemba Afloat

Serves 4

A good quantity of cleaned mussels

2 carrots

1 onion

4 cloves garlic

1 red chilli

A quantity of bechamel sauce

2 eggs

Bread crumbs

Oil for deep frying (preferably olive oil)

In a pan cook the mussels, no need to add water as the mussels have plenty of seawater, until they open about 3 - 5 minutes. Discard any mussels that don't open. Remove mussels from their shells, keeping the shells to one side. Chop mussels. Finely chop the onion, garlic, chilli, carrot and mussels and fry gently in a little olive oil. Make a thick bechamel sauce using butter, a couple of spoons of flour, salt and pepper and milk. It must be quite heavy. Add the mussel mixture to the bechamel and leave to cool. Beat 2 eggs in a shallow bowl and dip each stuffed mussel shell in the egg and then roll in breadcrumbs. Next, heat a good quantity of oil and deep fry the stuffed mussels. This takes a second until brown. Drain. Take the mussel shells and fill each half with a little of the mixture. Serve with quartered limes.

Saladi ya Juma

Serves 2

1 unripe pawpaw

4 cloves garlic, chopped

Good dash of thai fish sauce

1 green & 1 red chilli, de-seeded

Juice of 3 limes

1 tbs fresh coriander, chopped

Salt

Grate the paw paw. Mix in all other ingredients and a good dash of thai fish sauce. Refrigerate to cool. Serve.

Warm octopus salad

Serves 4

1 large octopus

Juice of 3 limes

Olive oil

6 large cloves garlic

Freshly ground pepper

3 onions

Salt

1 lettuce, shredded

First, catch your octopus and tenderise it. Boil in seawater until really tender and leave to cool. When cool skin and slice. Chop garlic and slice onions. Take a little olive oil and fry garlic, add octopus, turning continually. Turn up heat and add onions and plenty of freshly ground pepper. Add onions and cook for a minute or so, add lime juice and then serve on a bed of shredded lettuce.

**Many thanks to the following managers
and chefs for contributing the recipes that appear in this book:**

Mark at Bluebay, Nicolas at Blues, Nathalie at Breezes and The Palms, Patrick and Gilly at Chapwani, Deborah at Chumbe Island, Waldemar and Stefanie at the Dhow and Mtoni Marine restaurants, Chris at Emerson & Green and Kidude, Hannes at Fundu Lagoon, Maura at Imani Beach Villa, Jan at Karafuu Hotel, Chef Roy at the Zanzibar Serena Inn and Mangapwani, Peter at Mapenzi Beach Club, Jane and Alastair at Matemwe Bungalows, Mike and Zara at Mbweni Ruins, Ismail at Mercury's Restaurant, Geoff and Emanuelle at Mnemba Island, Philip and Charlie at Pemba Afloat, Dukey at Ras Nungwi Beach Hotel, Laurence at Sultan Palace hotel, Abdul at Tembo House Hotel, and Butch at Zanzibar Beach Resort.

Thanks also to Mervin Mah and Frankie Tan in Singapore, to Sean Qureshi of Spectrum Colour Lab in Nairobi, to Bobby McKenna for proof editing, to Terence, Ali and Antony here at Zanzibar Gallery Publishers, to Zarina Jafferji for allowing us to use her recipes in the Forodhani Gardens chapter, and to Kulsum and Abid and Bashira Jafferji for their help and support.

Contact Addresses

Bluebay Beach Resort
PO Box 3276, Zanzibar
Tel: +255 24 2240240/1/2
Mobile: +255 (4)747 413323/
413817
Fax: +255 24 2240245
Email: bluebay@twiga.com

Blues Restaurant
PO Box 2154, Zanzibar
Tel: +255 24 2236211/2
E-mail: blues@halcyon.co.tz

Breezes Beach Club
PO Box 1361, Zanzibar
Tel: +255 741326595
Fax: +255 741333151
Email: breezes@africaonline.co.tz
www.breezes-zanzibar.com

Chapwani Private Island
PO Box 3248, Zanzibar
Tel: +255 744 858111
Email: chapwani@zitec.org

Chumbe Island Coral Park (CHICOP)
PO Box 3203, Zanzibar
Tel/Fax: +255 24 2231040
UK: fax +44 (0)870 1341284
Email: chumbe@zitec.org
www.chumbeisland.com

The Dhow Restaurant
PO Box 992, Zanzibar
Tel: +255 24 2250117
Tel: +255 747 430117
Email:mmr@zanzinet.com

Emerson and Green
236 Hurumzi Street
PO Box 3417, Zanzibar
Tel: +255 747 423266
Fax: +255 747 429266
Email: emerson&green@zitec.org
www.zanzibar.org/emegre

Fundu Lagoon
PO Box 3945, Pemba
Tel: +255 24 2232926
Tel: +255 741 326551/3
Fax: +255 741 326552
Email: fundu@africaonline.co.tz
www.fundulagoon.com

Imani Beach Villa
PO Box 3248, Zanzibar
Tel: +255 24 2250050
Email: info@imani.it
www.imani.it

Karafuu Hotel
PO Box 71, Zanzibar
Tel +255 741325757
Fax: +255 741325670
Email: karafuu-hotel@twiga.com
www.karafuuhotel.com

Kidude Restaurant
PO Box 3417, Zanzibar
Tel: +255 24 2230171
Tel: +255 747 423266
Fax: +255 24 2231038
Email: emegre@zanzibar.org
Email: emerson&green@zitec.org
www.zanzibar.org/emegre

Mangapwani Seafood Grill and Watersports
PO Box 4151, Zanzibar
Tel: +255 24 2233587
Fax: +255 747 333170

Mapenzi Beach Club
Planhotel Zanzibar Ltd
PO Box 100, Mahonda, Zanzibar
Tel: +255 741 324985/325985
Tel: +255 747 414268
Fax: +255741333739
Email: resa@planhotelzanzibar.com
www.planhotelzanzibar.com

Matemwe Bungalows
PO Box 3275, Zanzibar
Tel: +255 747 425788
Fax: +255 747 429788
Email: info@matemwe.com
www.matemwe.com

Mbweni Ruins
PO Box 2542, Zanzibar
Tel: +255 24 2235478
Fax: +255 24 2230536
Email: hotel@mbweni.com
www.mbweni.com

Mercury's Restaurant
PO Box 3435, Zanzibar
Tel: +255 24 2233076
Tel: +255 747 416666
Fax: +255 24 2237314
Email: mercury's@zanzinet.com

Mnemba Island
PO Box 3107, Zanzibar
Tel: +255 741 326575
Email: mnemba@zitec.org
www.ccafrica.com

Mtoni Marine Restaurant
PO Box 992, Zanzibar
Tel: +255 24 2250117
Tel: +255 747 430117
Email:mmr@zanzinet.com

The Palms
PO Box 1298 Zanzibar
Tel: +255 741326595
Fax: +255 741333151
Email: bookings@tourafrica.ke
www.palms-zanzibar.com

Pemba Afloat
PO Box 117, Wete, Pemba
Tel: +255 748 341459
Email:
pembaafloat@pembaisland.com
www.pembaisland.com

Ras Nungwi Beach Hotel
PO Box 1784, Zanzibar
Tel +255 24 2233767/2232512
Fax: +255 24 2233098
Email: rasnungwi@zanzibar.net
www.rasnungwi.com

Zanzibar Serena Inn
PO Box 4151, Zanzibar
Tel: +255 24 2233587
Fax: +255 24 2233019
Email: zserena@zanzinet.com
www.serenahotels.com

Sultan Palace Hotel
Relais and Chateaux
PO Box 4074, Zanzibar
Tel: +255 24 2240173
Fax: +255 24 2240188
Email: info@sultanzanzibar.com
www.sultanzanzibar.com

Tembo House Hotel
PO Box 3974, Zanzibar
Tel: +255 24 2232069/2233005
Fax: +255 24 2233777
Email: tembo@zitec.org

Zanzibar Beach Resort
PO Box 4770 Zanzibar
Tel: +255 747 417782-4
Fax: +255 747 417785
Email:
enquiries@zanzibarbeachresort.com
www.zanzibarbeachresort.com

The Photographer

Javed Jafferji studied photography, film and television in the UK, before returning to Tanzania to publish various books, including Historical Zanzibar - Romance of the Ages; Images of Zanzibar; Zanzibar Stone Town - an Architectural Exploration; Zanzibar - an Essential Guide; Tanzania - African Eden, A Taste of Zanzibar, Zanzibar Style, Safari Living, and Safari Living Recipes.

His work has been published in national and international newspapers and magazines including The Times, Newsweek and Geo. He has held exhibitions in London, Paris, Berlin and Pakistan as well as Tanzania.

Javed also publishes a magazine called 'The Swahili Coast' to promote eco-tourism in Zanzibar and Pemba, manages a photography and design studio and runs a gift shop, the Zanzibar Gallery, which sells gifts, clothes, books and antiques.

The Stylist

Kulsum Jafferji, Javed's wife, runs the Zanzibar Gallery, a bookshop and craft gallery in the heart of Zanzibar's Stone Town. Her interest in food styling developed over the course of many photographic trips with Javed to Tanzania's best hotels, lodges and safari camps.

The Writer

Gemma Pitcher fell in love with Africa when she was seventeen and has been returning as often as possible ever since. She studied English Literature at Exeter University, UK, and worked as a safari consultant and editor before starting a career as a freelance travel writer. She has contributed to the *Bradt Guide to Zanzibar* and written articles for several international magazines as well as authoring the title *Zanzibar Style*.

Zanzibar Style, also by Javed Jafferji and Gemma Pitcher, was voted one of the 'Top 20 Travel Books for Christmas 2001' by the UK's Times newspaper.